LIFE-A CREATIVE ADVENTURE

Lance Heard

To my beautiful Friend Curt.
The memories of what you mean To me
in my life and heart will go on For
all eternity and eternity is a very
long time my Friend.
"I Love you with all my heart."

Looking Forward To having more memories,
Seeing you and having Fun in The Future in
unlimited ways......
You're buddy. Lance

ISBN: 0692473777
ISBN 13:9780692473771

Library of Congress Control Number: 2015910053

TABLE OF CONTENTS

Acknowledgments. vii
Introduction. ix

Chapter 1: Self-Love. 1
The attributes of choosing inner Self-love 1
Self-love and health 2
Self-love heals the world 3
Self-love technique. 4
Self-love meditation 5

Chapter 2: Addictions and their influences. 7
How to discover addictions by using the mirror. 8
Breaking away from addictions by letting go. 9
How to use addictions as a tool. 11
Using triggers as a tool 11
Meditations: Healing addiction by anchoring inner love 13
        Self-love meditation for addictions. 13
        Sound meditation for addictions. 13
        Mirror meditation for addictions. 14
Test to see if you have healed an addiction. 14

Chapter 3: How to eliminate childhood triggers. 16
Asking Higher Self and angels for help 17
The different facets of love. 18
Healing the ten-generation plague 20
Releasing the middleman 22
How to find trapped children by using your feelings 22
Exercise: Finding the Child Using the String Technique 24
How to find trapped children by using triggers as a tool 24
Exercise: Integrating fragmented children 25
Integration meditation. 26

Chapter 4: Why growth feels so hard 29
Embracing the darkness through surrender. 30
Letting go of old stuck energy 31
Allowing for patience and love. 33

Chapter 5: The facets of Oneness 34
Understanding the Oneness in everyday life 35
Finding answers in your employment circumstances. 37
The key to enlightenment is to lighten up. 39
The Oneness is you! 39
More lessons on Oneness 44

Chapter 6: Creators, not victims 46
Luck has nothing to do with it 46
Our thoughts have the ability to create. 47
What you focus on, is what you get 49
Practice makes perfect 50

Chapter 7: How words create our reality 52
How words can anchor into our consciousness 54
Creating new word patterns 55
Starving the old synapses 57
Living your new reality. 58

Chapter 8: How healing works 60
The two primary healing chakras and how to use them 61
Healing through sound 62
Healing through movies 64
Healing through art forms. 65
Healing through the hands and eyes. 66
Healing through the Oneness 67
Healing through button-pushing and triggers. 69
You are the creator of your own healing techniques. 70
Belief is necessary for healing 71

Chapter 9: Diving in & cleansing 74
Diving into the darkness to find the light 74
Exercise: The string technique 75
Healing past-life triggers. 76
Exercise: Releasing past-life issues 77
The deeper realities of healing 78
Going through the process of healing. 80
Go slowly when releasing. 81
Definition of the cleansing process. 82
The art of cleansing. 83
Tourniquet to ease cleansing. 84

Chapter 10: How stones heal 85
Stones are alive. 86
Exercise: Clearing stones and crystals 86
Selenite: the healing stone 87
Selenite for meditation 88
Meditation with selenite 89
How to create a vortex for meditation 90

Chapter 11: Dreams and their significance 91
The different facets of dreams. 92
The power of symbols. 92
Symbolic dreams. 93
Soul-traveling dreams. 96
Contact dreams 98
Visitation dreams 99
Programming your dream book 100

Chapter 12: Past lives and their influences 102
A vision of the past. 103
Encountering my spirit guide 104
Nurturing the seeds of past lives. 106
The secrets of the past are revealed 108
The power of setting past lives free 109

Chapter 13: The bondage of judgment 112
Judgment makes us stuck 112
Learning to transmute judgment. 113
Choosing to let go of judgment. 115
Exercise: Technique to release judgment 116
We have to go through the dark to get to the Light. 118
Through calamity we can find the Oneness 119

Chapter 14: The effects of war 122
Planet Earth is alive 122

Chapter 15: When we die 124
Death means a new experience. 124
We create our own death. 126
We leave our bodies when we sleep 127
My meditation 128

Chapter 16: When a person commits suicide 131
A letter to my client about suicide 133
Helping loved ones into the Light. 135
The power of God-Words 138

Chapter 17: How to make contact with our
                    star-born ancestors. 140
Asking for ET help 141
ET implants. 142
Technique: how to establish contact with ETs 144
The Plejarens are here! 145
Be patient with yourself 146

About the Author. 148
Recommended Regression Hypnotherapist 149

ACKNOWLEDGMENTS

I'm extremely grateful and thankful for my beautiful loving wife, Silvia Teresa Gallo Vazquez, for her love and support in writing this book, for allowing me to be myself and for the lessons she taught me in what it means to truly love and to be loved. I am extremely grateful for the family, friends and acquaintances in my life and for the reflections they presented to me, to help me grow. If it weren't for their mirror, the journey would have been a lot harder.

Special thanks to Barbara Becker, Summer Bacon, Dr. Peebles, Susan Palmer and the angels and guides, for helping me through my life process.

I love you all dearly.
Lance

INTRODUCTION

I was born in 1961, in a place I would refer to back then as a mosquito town named El Centro, California. Needless to say, most anybody who has lived or lives there now, will tell you it's a very hot and humid, mosquito-infested farmland paradise created by the layer of fertile suet left over from the receding waters of the Colorado River, created by the affects from the construction of the Hoover Dam between 1931 and 1936.

When I was a kid growing up in El Centro, I thought abuse, in the form of harsh words and heavy hands, was a natural way of life. I actually didn't think anything of it. It wasn't until later in life when I started dealing with the emotional scars and abuse left behind in its wake, I began wondering why everything I did in life never seemed to work for me.

When I noticed my life was always one disaster after another, while at the same time being bombarded with thoughts raging through my head of, "Nobody loves me, everybody just wants to take advantage of me and what's the point of even trying and it doesn't matter anyway." So, when I got much older in life, I realized that having all of these thoughts was kind of a big bummer. "Why in the heck do I feel this way?" I asked myself.

After asking this question, that night I had a dream. In the dream, the angels took me to a place that had a big white fence around it with two large French doors open to reveal its other side. After I was allowed to gaze behind its walls, an angel said to me, "This is where people who are severely abused live." I began looking around at the houses and its streets. It looked like a place that was bombed and burned down; like the poorest place a person could possibly live.

It was only after this dream, I felt like a light switch flipped on. I experienced a huge wave of unstoppable feelings and forgotten thoughts from my childhood, as they rushed into my awareness. As I was feeling the existence of their presence inside of me, then realized how severely abused I had been as a child and thought, "How in the hell am I going to get out of this place?" I said to myself, "Even if I had a worst enemy, it would make me feel extremely sad to think that they would even have to spend a minute here."

My abuse as a child made it very difficult for me to trust people. I realized in order for me to get the purest answers without the influence of the world's perceptions in how to heal myself, I would have to try something out of the box. So, I asked myself, "How did Jesus do it?" The answer I got was that he trusted that when he asked his father for a fish, he wouldn't be fed a scorpion. So, I decided to do it the old-fashioned way. I knew I was working with angels. I decided I would just ask them for help in showing me how to get out of this big mess I was in. I said to myself, "I just need to make a decision and believe how a child would, with one hundred percent trust, that I wouldn't be given a scorpion when I ask for the answer to my questions."

I began every day being honest with myself and looking deep inside of me. Systematically going down the line of each of my issues and asked the angels to help me by any means possible. This help could be in my dreams, or whatever it takes, so I could understand why all of this happened to me and so, they did. I used the insights they gave me to heal myself. Then it dawned on me. I bet there are a lot of people on this planet who have gone through the same things; thinking that it was a normal way of life to be abused and they don't even know that abuse is abnormal. Hence, this book was created, a record of the answers that set me free from my abusive childhood.

CHAPTER 1

Self-Love

In order to find inner love and set ourselves free from our addictions and destructive behaviors, we must first be aware of the energetic direction in which love flows and come to the conclusion that we will never find love coming from the outside in. It will always come from the inside out. This mere awareness of the direction that love moves in, will easily reveal hidden addictions and behaviors. It will stop a plethora of undesirable situations from taking hold in the first place. The other thing that inner love does, is that as it grows in you. From using Self-love techniques, love will automatically show you what needs to be done inside of your consciousness. This is because Self-love doesn't resonate with any false emotional or undesirable perceptions of love.

The attributes of choosing inner Self-love

The very first thing I recommend doing before procuring any type of self-help healing modality, would be learning Self-love. The reason why I recommend doing this first, is because of the mass array of benefits that Self-love provides, such as, accepting yourself exactly the way you are and being patient with yourself. It eliminates beating yourself up and doesn't allow others to put you down or beat you up verbally or physically. You no longer want to stay in an abusive relationship any longer than necessary, because that is not what love would want. You eat better and exercise more. You take naps, when necessary, go out and have some fun in life, attract more friends and live a more balanced life in general.

If you don't love yourself, one may have a tendency to look for a partner to complete themselves and have a tendency to stay in abusive relationships for way too many years than necessary or use relationships as an addiction. You go from one relationship to another, hoping to find your true love and then terminate the relationship after the drug wears off. Then you get right back into another relationship, again and again. My angels told me in a dream, "Love yourself, know yourself and marry yourself, before you can marry somebody else." The key here in having Self-love before getting into a relationship, is that it already provides all the inner fulfillment of love, happiness and acceptances, you'll ever need in life and it lasts forever inside of you, instead of fading away like addictions do. So that means, that absolutely nobody coming into your life from the outside can give you what you don't already have on the inside. Knowing you already have everything you ever wanted, is extremely powerful, because it will give you the awareness to make healthy choices before deciding to get into a relationship.

Finding inner Self-love doesn't mean you only love yourself and don't care about the other people on the planet or in your life. On the contrary, it magnifies your relationship with yourself and others; by having more compassion for yourself and others, accepting yourself and others and giving loving allowance for yourself and others. Always put yourself first, when pertaining to Self-love, because you can't give what you don't already have. Everything ascertained from the outside-in, after first ascertaining Self-love, will be like frosting on the cake!

Self-love and health

Self-love is the best diet on the planet when it comes to losing weight and becoming healthy. It does this without feeling guilty for being overweight or not exercising and will encourage you to do it without even having anybody to tell you that you need to do it. Self-love just has a way of creeping up on you and has a consciousness of its own. For example, without judgment, shame or beating one's self up, it will teach you what and not what to eat or drink. It will teach you the need to exercise and be kinder to yourself. You will accept yourself the way you are when you are going through your processes and to be patient with yourself. Self-love will lovingly give you the encouragement and energy necessary to want to follow through with whatever is necessary to bring you to your desired health.

Self-love heals the world

I believe that Self-love will eventually generate the driving force required by the Oneness, to create the desired ripple effects necessary to completely heal our beautiful and loving home called planet Earth. [I will cover the concept of the Oneness more in-depth in Chapter 5.] Just think, if we all or a large percentage of the population, made a choice to love themselves, then we wouldn't want to eat polluted food, drink polluted water or breath polluted air. In fact, we as a whole, would demand that we clean up the planet and the cool thing is, we would do it in a loving way because Self-love would be leading the way to discover unique ways to eliminate our addictions to over-consume. We wouldn't associate love with having stuff anymore. The ripple effects of eliminating over-consumption, would create an automatic change, because the powers that be, meaning the one percentiles of the population that created the way they wanted us to act and feel, through media and other means, would be challenged to come up with a solution to fit the direction on which the consciousness of the mass population is pointing. Part of their processes would likely be to shift their focus on nurturing the planet. After all, how would the powers-that-be, be able to keep their perception of how the economy is supposed to work and how money is supposed to work, if a large percentage of the population decided to leave a smaller footprint on the planet and not play by the old rules anymore? In my opinion, when the power of Self-love kicks in, we wouldn't even have to picket to save the planet anymore because we would be nurturing it out of love for ourselves. If suddenly, the powers-that-be began to lose all control over mass consumption and distribution of goods, because we chose to love ourselves and by doing so, we dissolved the illusion that buying stuff, (coming from the outside in) will make us have more love or make us feel better about are lives. Then they will lose the power to feed our addictions through the pill they feed us called "over-consumption." We will finally defeat the old paradigm by using love instead of the old ways of fighting and anger. We would set ourselves free from over-consumption, which will ultimately lead to Mother Earth being able to heal herself. The processes of imbalance would decline in and on Mother Earth, including birth defects, health issues, imbalances in humans, stress, inflammatory issues and our combined sadness with Mother Earth.

Through our interconnectedness to the Oneness, imbalance will cease to exist. The other cool thing about Self-love, is that it will help us have more compassion for others. It will give us abilities to lift others up, instead of pulling them towards us or down. Meaning, if we see others in a state of frustration, Self-love will give us the ability to have more compassion for others, because the compassion for ourselves, leads and teaches us the to see others as ourselves, instead of belittling others (pulling others towards us) or trying to make others feel the way we might feel about ourselves, because of our own insecurities.

If you are serious about having inner Self-love, peace, balance, fulfillment, a healthy relationship with self and with others, you must do your part to help the planet and contribute to ending war, through Self-love. I recommend practicing the Self-love techniques provided in this book.

Self-love technique

Some of us, as we grew up, may not have had the happiest experiences in life because we were always looking for recognition and acceptance from the outside in, meaning; coming from somebody other than ourselves to give us the love, recognition, happiness and the respect, we all deserve. In order to release the old drama, we held onto and be able to forgive others for what we perceived they did to us, we must give to ourselves what we wanted others to give us. One of the techniques I like to use is affirmations. Affirmations are well-chosen power words designed to create their unique energetic frequency inside of your consciousness which will ultimately lead to creating a desired inner feeling. I recommend that the first thing you do when you wake up in the morning is to start repeating these words for no less than twenty minutes a day or as often as possible, especially if you start feeling frustrated during the day:

"I love myself the way I am. I feel extremely happy with my life. I am grateful that I have everything I need in my life. I accept myself the way I am. I am in my power. I am in balance. Today, is a day full of magic and I feel excited about my life!"

Using these affirmations will raise your vibration and will eventually cause the feelings they create to become a permanent fixture. Eventually, you won't have to repeat the words as often, as you used to, because you will simply become the words and the feelings they resonate with. Remember, heaven isn't a place you go when you die, it's a feeling. You can go as high as you want to heaven. It's up to you.

Self-love meditation

Sit in a chair and tell yourself, "It is time to relax now." Begin taking slow, long, deep breaths, only in the solar plexus area. (By the way, deep breathing is a form of communication to yourself and the universe proclaiming your willingness to trust, embrace, surrender and receive divine healing.) Then, in your third eye, located a little up and between the eyebrows, imagine yourself growing really big, so big, you see yourself in space looking down at the earth. Then, bring a violet light coming down from way out in space down to the top of your head and pull it down through your crown chakra located on the top of your head. Keep pulling the light down until it goes into your heart. Feel your heart expanding like a balloon filling up inside of you. When you feel your heart is at full capacity, release the energy down through your whole body. See and feel yourself levitating. It is important while doing this meditation to keep your focused attention in your heart. Breathing deeply, feel the light passing through you and the sensation of levitating all at once.

This is a meditation I received through my dreams. It tremendously helped me to open my heart. I recommend using this meditation every day for a minimum of twenty minutes a day or at night, before you go to sleep, for the rest of your life, to see how far you can go and how much love will be revealed to you. It's very exciting to know that there is no "there" to get to, because where you are, you are going to get to, next. This meditation will help you, especially when it comes to receiving, giving and understanding more ways to love. You will experience love in ways beyond your wildest dreams and imaginations.

Although, I love myself, I found we all have addictions to help us cope in this life. Addictions are another area that I needed to address, in order for me to go forward.

Chapter 2

Addictions and their influences

Addictions come from associating things such as drugs, food, objects, actions, reactions and so on, with what we perceive to be feelings of love, happiness, joy and peace. The question is, why do we have addictions in the first place? Addictions come from feelings of the inner lack of love.

What we're really looking for, are the feelings of love that addictions simulate inside of us. But the truth is, an addiction is like a pill after you consume it; it only lasts for a few hours. When the drug wears off, the old patterns that caused us to take the drug in the first place, begin to creep back into our lives, which leads us right back to where we started from. This keeps us going around and around in circles and where we stop, nobody knows. The key here lies in understanding, what it is we are *truly* looking for. What will fill the big seemingly never-ending void inside of us? That thing, is inner love and the discovery in the direction love flows.

For example: Taking illegal drugs, over-consumption of food, sex, store bought products and anything done obsessively, that is brought from the outside in and is used to generate temporary feelings of love, happiness, peace and joy, after a period of time, their influence over us wears off and we fall back into despair and pain. This is revealing an illusion in the form of an addiction. Being aware of these patterns ultimately gave me the incentive to heal my addictions, especially when I realized that if I didn't, how I would be trapped, possibly for the rest of my life, in my chosen addictions.

How to discover addictions by using the mirror

Many years ago, at a time in my life when I was barely beginning to consciously understand the multifaceted existences of the Oneness, I observed in judgment, a person sitting on a park bench who I knew was a heroin addict. I asked myself, "How could he do that to himself? What a waste of his potential!"

Then, as quick as I used my judging words, a thought came to me that said, "That's you." Then the inner voice followed through by saying, "He is presenting to you a reflection of yourself, revealing your addiction to judgment, so that you can learn how judgment has stopped you from reaching your full potential. He is doing this, out of love for you." When the truth of the mirror and my addiction to judgment was revealed to me through my interaction with this heroin addict, I started crying like a little baby, because I realized how much we truly love each other. I then thanked him inside of my head and said, "How grateful I am for the gift he gave me, in revealing the mirror and for helping me to become aware of its reflections." Becoming aware of this form of communication the universe speaks to us through its reflection, helped me to come to the awareness of how much we are truly loved, how much of a gift we truly are and how important it is for each one of us to be here. We are here, not only for our energetic connections as one, but through the love that we give to one another through our reflection in the mirror, because after all, if there is only one, that means everything you see is truly you.

After this experience, I asked my angels, "How I can help myself and others heal their addictions in the best way possible?" The answer that came to me was,

"By accepting yours and the addictions of others as part of your life's process; without judgment. After all, everybody has addictions that come in many forms and all forms have the possibility of creating devastating effects. There is no difference between a heroin addict and anyone else."

Although this was a hard concept for me to embrace at the beginning, it became easier after I realized that the gift the heroin addict was giving me was in the form of a profound universal love communication, I call, *the reflection*. It wasn't until I could see the heroin addict as a reflection of me in the form of a mirror trying to help me see with compassion that we all have addictions. After seeing this, I thought, "At least he is being honest and not hiding his addictions like I am." In fact, I realized that what the heroin addict was doing for me by his reflection of me, was revealing that I had deep hidden addictions that were destroying my ability to receive the love, happiness, joy, abundance of prosperity and the peace, I deserved and longed for.

I believe if we make a choice to heal our addictions, the universe will no longer have to reflect to us in ways of despair through others that we have addictions. I believe this is how we can help heal the world. By healing ourselves, the ripple effect it creates will assist in healing not only planet Earth, but all its inhabitants which will ultimately lead to pristine inner love in all beings. Through Self-love, you just naturally see what needs to be done and want to take charge in making the changes; not because somebody is trying to force you to do it, but because you'll love yourself and will be on the automatic pilot of love.

On that note, just think what would happen if all people decided to take the time to find their hidden addictions and find the inner love that they've been longing for, their whole lives? I ask myself, "I wonder what the reflections would look like then?"

Breaking away from addictions by letting go

Addictions can be hard to break away from, because of the reflected circumstances and the individuals we've surrounded ourselves with, in order to reinforce our addictions and fulfill our self-inflicted prophecies. There are many ways to start the process toward healing addictions, that include consulting healers, psychologists and counselors.

Sometimes we might have to separate ourselves even temporarily from our loved ones during the time of healing. That doesn't mean we don't love them and accept them the way they are. In fact, it is the exact opposite. It is revealing to us how much of a lover we truly are. To me, temporarily letting go of a loved one is a form of Self-love, because deep inside, we know it's the right thing to do, at least for now. We realize in order for us to change, we have to recreate a new environment that matches the new realities we are trying to create. Being in that old environment isn't a positive influence and isn't pointing us toward our desired direction. I like to think of making a decision to create some needed space from a loved one as equivalent to making a decision not to watch certain episodes on TV, because of the influence they may have.

The cool thing about creating this space is that, although oftentimes it can be very painful, after we heal ourselves, we can choose to get back together again with those loved ones, if we so desire. Except this time, there will be a big difference. We will no longer have the addictions inside of us. Therefore, our loved ones will no longer trigger us to slip back into our old addictions. Another thing I noticed about giving some space in a relationship, it oftentimes will cause both parties to go into deep introspection, because each party won't be feeding each other's addictions anymore. When we interact with others after the split, we begin to realize the patterns we keep recreating. After we become aware that we are the ones creating the way we feel and interact with others, it causes us to take full responsibility for our life as a creator and have the incentive to take action in our self-growth.

Once these addictions are revealed, it then becomes our responsibility to release them. In the action of releasing old addictions, the true inner meanings of love that were buried behind our addictions will finally find their way to our awareness and out to the surface and begin to alter our perceptions of self and others, as they become anchored into our consciousness. In doing so, new concepts of love become our new realities.

It is at this point we will finally be able to allow our new forms of inner love to increase within us, as it begins to grow and reveals its inner hidden secrets. It will then project itself out into the world in forms such as: acceptance of ourselves, acceptance of others, our interactions with others, the reflection we present to others, the reflection others present to us and an increased awareness of love, way beyond our wildest dreams and imaginations. When we find Self-love and by releasing our addictions, there will be absolutely nothing the world can give us that we don't already have. Everything that comes into our lives from the outside in from this point on, will be the icing on the cake. In fact, if you want to think of love like a drug, then love will be the best drug we have ever had, because it never ends or loses its effects.

How to use addictions as a tool

Addictions can be an awesome tool when used in the process of self-discovery. The main thing here, is when learning to use addictions as a tool, I recommend trying to view them only as a tool to be used as a part of the process into self-discovery. Use them to show where your deep inner secrets are located through your repetitive patterns, instead of the old way that you've been taught here on the school called planet Earth; such as defining them as bad, disgusting, or something to be ashamed of. After all, we don't want to feed the old addictions of mass consciousness and hinder the rapid growth and expansion of love here, any longer than necessary; such as for thousands or more years. We are co-creators and connected to everyone and everything.

Using triggers as a tool

Triggers are some of the greatest tools and gifts for the inner discovery of hidden addictions, because of the rapid influx of emotions they create when their switch is turned on. These tentacles of emotions can now be followed to their hiding places because their existence has been discovered through the feelings generated in the form of a trigger.

Oftentimes, being triggered can be the worst time to try and find their connections to the past and in letting them go, simply because at the moment of being triggered, we can't see the forest through the trees. This awareness helped me to see that, in order to help myself more effectively and come from a more balanced perspective, I first needed to find a way to get rid of all my inner turmoil. What I found really worked well for me, was using little catch phrases and speaking them to myself such as:

"When I'm in my highest power, absolutely nothing will bother me. I am the Way, the Light and the Truth. I am whole. I am complete and never have I been the victim, but always the creator and it is through my choices and perceptions, I create my reality."

Another gold nugget that's good to reflect on is this: if somebody gets mad at me, it tells me more about that person than it does about me. The opposite is also true. If I get mad at somebody else, it tells me more about myself, than it does about him or her.

These foundational tools are created for the purpose of anchoring a pathway back to my desired reality. They lead me back to the truth of who I really am, so I won't think that the interactions I had with others that led to my disappointment was their fault. That way, when I go into inner reflections of myself to find out why I felt the way I did when certain situations occurred in my life, I don't have the deceiving energetic effects of feeling like I am a victim and blaming other people or situations for how I feel. This enables me to come from a clear space and be more honest with myself in regard to my inner feelings while I am searching for the truth.

The other thing that is cool about this process is it enabled me to begin to see how important it is to have interactions with others because of the reflections they present to me, coming from the Oneness perspective. For me, it shows how much I am truly loved. I realize that somebody loved me enough to take time out of their lives to be with me and reflect to me my hidden addictions revealed through my triggers. In my journey, this insight eventually led me to the gateway of forgiveness, which eventually set me free from feeling like the victim and revealed to me beyond a shadow of a doubt, that we are all connected. Wow, what a beautiful gift they gave me. They help set me free!

It is at this part in the chapter, I feel it would be a good time to introduce three different inner Self-love meditations that tremendously helped me to open the flood gates of love in my heart. Through this act of Self-love, I discovered my hidden addictions as love taught me how to heal them. By wrapping my addictions in love and having compassion for myself, because I'm going through my unique process by allowing the addictions to be set free, in their own space and time, without judgment.

Meditations: Healing addiction by anchoring inner love

So, let's get down to the nitty-gritty. Following are three techniques I used to help anchor and facilitate the growth of inner Self-love.

1. **Self-Love Meditation for addictions:** For one month, take twenty minutes every day, get comfortable in a chair, bed, or whatever works for you and close your eyes. Begin to deep breathe only using your solar plexus, not bringing the breath into your lungs. In other words, use diaphragmatic breathing. Then give yourself a big hug and hold your arms there for the entire five minutes. Continue the deep breathing and begin to repeat nonstop, inside of yourself or out loud (whichever feels comfortable), "I love myself."

2. **Sound Meditation for addictions:** For one month, take twenty minutes every day, get comfortable in a chair, bed, or whatever works for you and close your eyes. Begin to deep breathe only using your solar plexus, not bringing the breath into your lungs. Turn on some soothing music and begin to imagine an elevator in your brain with its door open, where you and your sound system

are inside of the elevator. Then watch the elevator door close and begin to feel it as it's moving down to your heart. When the elevator stops and the elevator door opens, imagine the sound blasting into your heart. Begin to listen to the music through your heart until your five minutes is over. This technique will bring what's in your mind down to your heart. Think of it like an exercise in a gym, as it's teaching you how to use and open your heart.

3. **Mirror Meditation for addictions:** Stand in front of a mirror naked. Begin the deep breathing techniques listed above and for twenty minutes, repeat these words: "I love myself the way I am." Do this every day for one month and if for some reason, there is a spot on your body you don't feel comfortable with looking at, focus on that area on your body and repeat, "I love myself the way I am. Love is magic in our lives. With love we can heal anything."

When you first utilize these techniques, you will often be consumed by feelings of doubt, fear and all kinds of negative thoughts. This is just the old you, trying to fight back and regain control. Push it out. Don't listen to it and keep going, no matter what. It will be well worth it. Utilizing any one of these three techniques will place a seed deep down into your soul as your words become the water, which causes it to grow naturally, revealing all of its inner secrets of Self-love.

Test to see if you have healed an addiction

One test I like to use to help me see when I have finally let go of an issue or addiction, is by comparing the way I used to interact and feel to my past interactions and feelings toward others in life, to my present feelings. I do this after coming home from a loved one's house, or after some time has passed, after I've given permission to my angels to heal certain discovered issues ferreted out by love. I start by going to my favorite chair and sit down while taking several deep breaths. Then I compare myself by reflecting on how different our present interactions are between each other, than they were in the past. When I first tried this technique, I was amazed in my discovery and said to myself, "Wow, that's amazing how our interactions with each other don't influence me anymore the way they used to. It feels like I have amnesia of the past!"

In fact, this is my number one tool to let myself know when I have healed myself from the past. However, there are issues and problems that started in my childhood. This became a focus of my healing and increasing my Self-love.

CHAPTER 3

How to eliminate childhood triggers

As most of us will agree, the biggest influence on the development of the etched-in integration of our beliefs came through repetitive speech patterns—the physical and mental interactions that began in our early childhood trauma with our parents and family members. It took me well into my early adult life before I began to realize the repeating undesirable effects of the physical and mental abuse in my early childhood and the role it played in my adult life. Growing up, I slowly started becoming aware of the destructive outcomes in my relationships, interactions and the influences I had with myself and others. Until this awareness grew to the point where I was starting to see that, in order for me to have the loving and happy life I wanted for myself, I needed to heal my childhood and create a new reality from scratch. I realized that if I didn't let go of my childhood past, I would just keep reinforcing my present actions and reactions, living in an illusion, thinking that my actions and reactions are coming from a place of truth, when they really are coming from my past experiences of my childhood trauma. After I reflected on my interactions with myself and others, I realized that my interactions really didn't make any sense to me. I realized my childhood triggers were causing me to have preconceived assumptions of what other people were thinking about me and caused me to do funny and irresponsible things, because of the fear my childhood recreated inside of me. I then realized these preconceived assumptions were all just inside my head and has been a major hidden force that has kept me in my childhood trauma and caused me to give and receive the same old crap over and over again in my life. I realized that if I don't take action and heal my childhood trauma, I could take it to the grave with me and this could cause me to never, till the day I die, be able to create the things I truly want in life, such as Self-love, happiness, joy and balance.

After realizing that if I don't let go of my past, I will always be in its bondage. I began crying my eyes out and said to myself, "I am going to do whatever it takes to release myself from my childhood bondage, because there is no way in hell, I am going to let any person on Earth, or anywhere else for that matter, take away my power from me!" After coming to the awareness that I needed to take my power back, by letting go of my childhood trauma, I began to realize that nobody really took my power away from me in the first place. Actually, I gave it away, without even knowing it! I was blind, but now, I see. This awareness is a prime example of the concept of: "Never were you the victim, but always the creator."

So, the question here is, how do I take my power back? I realized there was no way I could do it by myself, because my old belief systems wouldn't allow me to get the true answers to my questions. Due to the influence my old belief systems had on me, coming from the past, I knew I needed help. So, I did what I would normally do and ask my Higher Self (my inner guidance) and angels to help me.

I realized in order for me to let go of my childhood trauma, I needed to completely forgive and let go of all the bad memories and only focus on the good memories. Holding those up high, even if it's only one good memory, that is enough. By only focusing on the good memories, I like to think of that good memory equivalent to one grain of love. All it takes to heal a whole tribe, is love, the size of one grain of sand. The reason why I chose to let go of my childhood trauma, is so I could make a choice to only focus on the good parts of my life and only allow the energies they carried to influence what I wanted to bring up to the present and then restart my new life from this new self-established point.

Asking Higher Self and angels for help

I realized in order for me to get the purest answers possible, I had to find a way to bypass my old belief systems in order to find a new truth to put in the place of my old one. This is what I call getting past the old guard dogs in my consciousness. To get help, I started by sitting in my favorite chair and began deep breathing taking a minimum of three deep breaths in my solar plexus area and just completely relax. Then I said in a normal tone of voice to myself,

"I give my Higher Self and angel's permission on all levels of my consciousness to do whatever it takes to help me understand how my childhood traumas and their influences are affecting me. I create that any techniques or energetic adjustments that are necessary in order to help me in what it is I have created, be given to me, with no limitations and on all levels of my consciousness. So be it!"

The rest of this chapter is based on the insights and techniques I learned from asking for help to resolve my childhood trauma. I will go over how our childhood triggers interact with our realities. I will share techniques on how to heal them and let them go for ever.

"Once you truly heal something and let it go, it never, ever comes back." ~ *Lance Heard*

What we learn from are childhood influences us in our daily lives and interactions with others. Oftentimes, we get caught up in being victims, in allowing what others did or said to us from the past, to influence our lives to the point where we don't even know who we are anymore. It's as if we choose to live in the hornets' nest our whole life, where all we know is what goes on inside the hornets' nest and not even realizing there's a hole along the outside edge where can look out of and see all the pretty flowers and trees. For me, it wasn't until I discovered that love means something different to everybody. I began to realize the different facets of love and that there is a key to understanding the many facets of love. That key is loving allowance and non-judgment of others.

The different facets of love

To one person, if you gave them a hug and told them how much you loved them, they may respond by holding the hug for a longer period of time, in order to savor the feeling in the exchange of the energy of love, while replying back, "I love you too." On the other hand, you could hug a different person and tell them you love them and they would get all stiff and feel insecure, responding with, "What do you want from me? You only hug me and tell me you love me when you want something." In these two scenarios, the first person embraces love because they associate love with, joy, gratitude and acceptance. The person in the second scenario, may associate love with pain, suffering, betrayal and sorrow.

I believe it is important to take into consideration that there are multiple facets of what love means to each person on this planet. Understanding this and embracing this concept will help you to let go of the past, because after all, we can't change what another person believes love is; only they can, in their own space and time. The thing we can do is share, not force our perceptions of love onto others and through our example, teach a kind and supportive form of love.

Many of us grew up in an environment that associates love with pain. It's not that the individuals we grew up with were bad people, they just grew up learning what love was through the eyes of others. In some instances, thinking that the harder they hit you, or shouted at you, was how to express how much they loved you. Example: Let's say there is a young kid going over to a light socket and he or she begins to stick a screwdriver in it. A family member sees what is going on and runs over to stop it. At this point, the family member has two options of expressing love; both rendering a ripple effect that will stay with that child for life and may be passed onto their own family children, when they get older. One scenario is the person in charge of the safety of the child could rush over, grab the kid and say with concern, "No, please don't do that. You can get electrocuted and die or get hurt really bad. I am telling you this so that you don't get electrocuted, because I love you so much," and give the child a big hug, a kiss and say, "I am so happy you're okay." The second scenario could be the family member runs over to the child, swats him or her, causing the child to fly across the room and shouts, "You stupid idiot! How many times do I have to tell you not to do that?!!"

Both scenarios are forms of love and carry a ripple effect that could last for the rest of that child's life, except one form has the ability to bring in more assuring and confident ripple effects in the later development of the child's life. In contrast, the other will bring in low self-esteem, lack of self-confidence, shame, self-hate and fear of what other people think about him or her. I believe the more aggressive form of love is what is referred to in the Bible as the "ten-generation plague."

"The definition of being enlightened is when we can see and take responsibility of our thoughts and actions and become more aware of the ripple effects they create." ~ Lance Heard

Healing the ten-generation plague

It ultimately takes one person in the family chain to break the inherited plague. The key to healing the plague starts with searching for the possibilities and the utilization of new realities in any current situation.

The first step to this process is being aware that our loved ones just didn't understand what they were doing, so they gave us their absolute best opinion, best form of love and best help, based on what they learned from their own childhood years. Understanding this principle can motivate us to take the first step toward making the changes required for healing. Understanding is necessary in order to create a reality that is more suitable to our unique desires in life. This will ultimately lead to the desired action of forgiveness. In order to start the process of dissolving childhood trauma and experiencing forgiveness, we must essentially dive into the darkness and find out why we feel the internal pain and suffering we do. Diving into the darkness will reveal the stolen realities we integrated as our truth, from the perceptions of our loved ones.

In order to do this, we must take into consideration that we have the ability to re-create our own realities and foundational belief systems. In doing so, we will truly know who we are because of this conscious decision to re-create ourselves. One of the benefits of creating your desired realities lies in the strength of knowing who you are. It will make you unshakable. This is what I believe is meant by the parable, "Know thyself." If one knows himself or herself, it is easy to realize when one is not.

The sheer understanding that I have complete control and the ability to change my reality prompted me to ask the question, "How do I know whether the reality I'm creating is the best one for me?" And the response that came to me was to think of myself as a scientist trying to discover a way to do something. In my case, wanting to dissolve the illusion of separateness was foremost. Embracing the fact that when you're trying to create a new reality in your life, realize there came a point where you have to push a button or flip a switch, to test your creation to see if it works. Sometimes things just blow up and other times, they don't.

In the past, I used to beat myself up when my new realities blew up in my face and didn't come out the way I wanted them to. I would say things to myself like, "I can't believe I did that—how stupid of me." So, I gave those negative thought processes a name: "The Middleman." I called beating myself, the middleman, for the reason, in using humor to break the spell that beating myself had on me. My new saying now is, "Whoops! There I go, using the middleman again!" and then laugh. I decided that the best way to get the quickest response in life, is just to cut out the middleman. Like in business, when using the middleman everything cost more. In this instance, you pay more in the form of chemical and emotional imbalance, suffering, sorrow and placing yourself in denial of Self-love.

So, now if something blows up, while I'm trying to recreate, I just keep re-creating myself until I find the reality that best matches my highest desires of who I want to be. There is no right or wrong way. There is only the way. Each way is different for each person and so is our perception.

Releasing the middleman

For me, the biggest thing that creeps in when I'm going through my cleansing process is me calling myself, stupid. The tool I use to help get me back on track is: number one, catching myself in the act of calling myself stupid and number two, realizing there's nobody else calling me stupid, except me.

This is what I call, *telling myself the truth* and by telling myself the truth, it releases the bondage of what stupid means to me and gives me the opportunity to make a conscious decision to change my mind without any of my old negative mind chatter coming in and stealing the vital energy I could use to focus on the things that bring happiness into my life. This is what I believe is meant by the words, "the truth shall set you free." By admitting that I am the only one calling myself stupid, I am being truthful to myself and truth causes me to take responsibility for the feelings and emotions that I conjure by calling myself or thinking that I am stupid. By being truthful to myself and admitting that it's only me that thinks negative thoughts about myself, helps me to see with clarity, that in this case the word stupid is only an illusion and doesn't really exist.

The word "stupid" only exists as a definition from the misunderstandings and insecurities of myself and of others. Besides that, it's not an individual's intelligence quotient (IQ) that determines his or her intellect; it's that person's ability to channel pure divine self, to "tap into the big brain."

How to find trapped children by using your feelings

After contemplating my interactions, perceptions and reactions, with myself and others for several years, I realized there are connections to my childhood. I began to see I could use my uncomfortable feelings as a tool, instead of getting mad at myself. I realized by using my feelings as a tool, I could follow them and they would lead to the door of deep hidden secrets inside of me. All I needed to do was walk through the door revealed from my feelings. This form of becoming aware of the existence of a trapped child is only to be used for what lies hidden in the background. It will reveal itself to us through the whisper of our feelings. The reason why these children within us are so hard to find, is because they get buried so deep and have been held at arm's length for so long, from the fear they hide behind and because of the pain they hold onto. This pain is born in the past.

The fastest and easiest way I know to find a trapped child in one's subconscious, is to take a quick glimpse at our childhood past and find any dramatic situations that we remember, just as if it happened yesterday. Each one of these memories is equivalent to one child found. After finding each child, we write down on a piece of paper how old we were, what happened and how it made us feel.

For example, let's say a son at the age of fourteen years was helping his father by holding the ladder while he was trimming the overgrown branches of a palm tree. The son was looking down on the ground because debris from the tree was falling on top of him and he didn't want any of the debris to fall into his eyes. On the decent of the ladder, the father after trimming the tree, he began revving the chain saw and without regards to his son standing beneath him, the father brushes the running blade of the chain saw against his son's shoulder and when the son yells, "OUCH!" the father yells down in a laughing voice and says, "Well, you stupid idiot! Why don't you look, where you're standing?!" This story is the complete scenario of what happened to this child. So, when systematically finding children and starting with number one, giving a description of all the children you find, it's important to keep things as simple as possible. You are just looking for a reference point, even though you may know what the whole story is, for example: 1. Age fourteen, chain saw.

Exercise: Finding the Child Using the String Technique

For the trapped children that are harder to find because the impact of the situation that happened to them was so traumatic that you just wanted to sweep it under the carpet, so it could never be found again, I would recommend utilizing the following technique.

Start by sitting in a chair or laying down on a bed with your eyes closed. Ask yourself why you feel the way you do. At this moment, a string will appear. Simply grab onto the string and start pulling it toward you as to ferret out the closeness of its end by utilizing the increased emotional feelings to guide you closer to the truth. When the end of the string is at hand, you will find the child you've been looking for.

The way I know I have found the right child is by putting the child I found at the end of the string, side by side in my mind's eye with the present situation that triggered me to get emotionally upset in the first place. I then see if the feelings match. If they do, that means I found the right child. After you are created your list and have all of your children written down, it's time to integrate your children.

The only thing those fragmented children ever wanted was love, understanding and acceptance. From the life-altering situations that occurred within those early childhood years, feelings of being unaccepted, shameful, bad and not good enough, were created. Since the pain was too unbearable to mention, a part of our soul fragmented and began to exist at arm's length. These very acts of holding ourselves at arm's length is what creates our inability to love ourselves. By integrating these fragmented children, the ability to create and achieve inner Self-love will increasingly get stronger as each child is integrated.

How to find trapped children by using triggers as a tool

Triggers are not meant to be viewed as a bad thing or something to be ashamed of. They are designed to be used as a tool, utilized in the process to guide one to self-discovery. For example: If you have a conversation with somebody and that person triggers you, it reveals to you that there is a fragmented child hiding in its wake. (I like to think of a trapped child as equivalent to a compact disc or computer file, floating around in your aura) and the trigger that activates the child and brings it to the surface in forms such as the way somebody looks at you, pats you on the back, raises an eyebrow, smiles at you, etc. (I see these triggers as the on-button on the compact disc player), as its being pushed from the fingers of our triggers, it begins to play the old childhood song or story from our past. What I see when our buttons are pushed, is that we literally trance-channel that old child from the past. You'll even act like that child and talk like him or her.

When we fragment a child, that's equivalent to telling a child, "Nobody loves you; not even me." By integrating a child, it's equivalent to saying to the child, "I love you exactly the way you are, you have never done anything wrong and from now on, I'm going to take care of you. You are safe here; you can be whatever you want to be and I will support you." It is important to integrate our trapped children, because they cause us to utilize too much of the vital life-force energy needed to be more focused and utilized for living our life's purpose.

Exercise: Integrating fragmented children

This technique is a form of self-hypnosis. Normally, when somebody comes to me for a healing session regarding the stuck children who are creating havoc in that person's adult life, this is the technique I use. You can either have somebody help you with this by reading it to you, or you can do it yourself.

Before I start any technique, I like to call in the angels and healers from the other side to help. I start off by saying out loud,

"I am here now to integrate this child I have found from the past. I give my angels, guides, star-born ancestors, or whoever can help me, permission on all levels of my consciousness to help me to integrate this child with no limitations. So be it!"

Integration meditation

Next, either sit in a chair or lay down on a bed face up and place your left hand on your solar plexus and the right hand on your heart. With your eyes closed, take several deep breaths using only the solar plexus. Try to consciously be aware of your breathing. This is very important as part of the healing process.

Start by imagining yourself inside of an elevator below the Root chakra, located beneath the groin area. See the door close as the elevator moves up and then stops at the Root chakra located at the groin area. The door opens and a red light comes in, filling up the whole inside of the elevator. Breathe in the color red, see it and feel it flowing into your body. Start feeling more relaxed as you take three deep breaths, breathing in the red light and filling the entire inside of your body.

Then, see the elevator door close and the elevator starts moving up again. As the elevator stops just below your belly button, the door opens and an orange light comes in. This is your Sacral chakra. Breathe in its soothing essence deeply three times, leading you even more into a peaceful and relaxed state.

Now the elevator's door closes and it starts moving up to your Solar Plexus chakra. The elevator stops just above your belly button, the door opens and a bright yellow ray of light like the sun comes flooding in. Feel it touching your skin. Begin to breathe it in deeply three times, feeling even more relaxed.

Now the elevator door closes, it starts moving up and then it stops at your Heart chakra. The door opens and at your heart, an emerald, green light that's even more soothing and relaxing comes into the elevator. Take three deep breaths here.

Now the door closes and the elevator starts moving up. The elevator stops at the Throat chakra area. The door opens and a light the color of aqua blue comes rolling in and filling the elevator. Begin feeling even more peaceful and relaxed at this time and continue deep breathing.

Then the door closes, the elevator starts moving up, the elevator stops at the Third Eye chakra, located just in the center of the forehead, just above the eye brows, the door opens and an indigo light comes pouring in as you take another three deep breaths. Here, you are feeling totally at peace and safe now.

The elevator door closes, the elevator moves up, the elevator stops at the top of the Crown chakra, at the top of your head, the door opens and a violet light comes in, filling the compartment. Take three more deep breaths.

Finally, the elevator door closes, the elevator moves up and stops just above the head, the door opens and a bright white light comes in. Begin walking toward the door of the elevator. Looking out in front of you, notice that there is a long hallway full of white light. Step out of the elevator and walk toward the door down the hallway.

As you are walking down the hallway, you see a white sign radiating of light with black letters hanging on the door of pure white light, with the words, "Reading the Past" on it. Reach down and open the door. As you walk into the room, there is the child you've been looking for. He or she looks exactly the same way you did at that age in your life.

Walk up to the child and start talking to him or her, convincing the child to come toward you. Introduce yourself by saying, "I am you from the future. I've come to get you and take care of you. What happened to you here wasn't your fault and you did nothing wrong. I have a room for you where you can live. You'll be safe and will always be loved and never judged. Please come with me." Then take the child by the hand and start walking out the door back into the hallway, back into the elevator.

The elevator door closes again and starts going down and then it stops at the Heart chakra level. The door opens and a green light comes in.

As you look out the elevator door, you see another hallway. It is called, "The Hallway to Your Heart." Walk hand in hand with your child. You'll see a door there at the end of the hallway. Open it and walk into the room. This is a beautiful room and it has a comfortable bed in it.

Now, tell the little child, "From this day forward, this is where you will live. I am going to be the one who takes care of you. You can be whatever you want to be. I will always love you. You will always be safe here and nobody will ever harm you again."

Now tell the child, "It's time for you to go to sleep now." Then take the child over to the bed inside of the room. After you watch the child get into bed, begin to pull the covers up. Kiss the child on the cheek and say how much you love him or her and tell the child that he or she can go to sleep now.

After you see the child close his or her eyes and begin sleeping in the bed, it is time to stand up, walk back out the door and close it behind you. Walk back down the hallway, to the elevator and step inside. See the door close and the elevator begin to move down. The elevator descends all the way to the bottom. It stops down below your Root chakra, right below your groin area. As the door opens, you know it's time to begin waking up and bring your consciousness back into the room where you are laying down or sitting and open your eyes. This concludes this technique of integration. I recommend going systematically down your list and integrating every child you have found using this technique.

This technique can be very powerful. After you are done, test yourself to see if it took, by using the connection between the trigger and the feelings it generated that revealed its existence to you in the first place. If you can no longer find any connection from triggers to the feelings and the connections to them, then congratulations, you did it. The reason childhood integration meditation works so well is because it gives *love* to the part of you that fragmented something it always wanted. Our perceptions of our inner work and integration of our wounds, can pose a challenge for us.

CHAPTER 4

Why growth feels so hard

More times than not, growth is a part of our life's process that we dread going through because of the internal pain and the suffering we experience while moving through it. I have come to realize that in order for me to move into my new desired reality, part of the process requires me to go through this growth and experience these feelings in order to find the freedom I am seeking.

In the past, I thought, "Does it always have to be this way? Why is it that every time I want to make a change in my life, I have to go through all this pain and suffering? Why does it always feel so hard?" And the answer I got was, "Because of what you associated your feelings with, while you were experiencing the growth: things such as guilt, shame and fear, all leading to the past, like the tentacles on an octopus. Also, it was because of how you spoke to yourself, as you were going through your growth. You would beat yourself up by saying, "When I am going to get it?" and, "When am I going to be done with this?"

As I came to realize that growth is inevitable, this led to the next question, "How can I go through growth in a more peaceful and loving way, so it doesn't feel like it's dragging me down so much?" The answer came to me just too simply: "Accept growth as part of your expansion process." In order for the growth process not to have such a strong hold on our emotions, reactions and actions, we must be able to embrace it, love it and accept it as part of the process.

I like to think of growth like the weather. Some days it's raining, other days the sun is out and other times the wind is blowing. The key here is to detach by not giving growth a form, or definition, because of its connections to the past.

Example: Let's say you are an adult in life and you're driving down a road high in the mountains and it's snowing. All of a sudden, you get a flat tire and realize you have to go out in the snow and change it. While you're changing your tire, you say to yourself, "Man its cold out here!" And all of a sudden, boom, you're going crazy. Just by using the word "cold" your unique definition of what cold means to you, will kick in and start growing tentacles to the past and connect to when you were a child. It could be that you accidently got locked out of your house in the snow for forty-five minutes and got frostbit and your parents had to take you to the hospital. For this very reason, I recommend detaching from defining what growth is, to eliminate the tentacles and the connection to your past experiences.

In this scenario, in order to detach, when this person had to stop the car and go outside in order to fix the tire in the snow, instead of saying its cold he or she, could have said, "It just is." By saying, "It just is" the word cold will no longer have definition and all of a sudden it just becomes a feeling on the skin and that's all it is, which will translate into a more relaxed feeling inside. This will cause a person's actions to be focused, save energy and be calculated. So, now if we chose to detach when we're going through our cleansing processes, we won't have to sit around for hours trying to figure out why our rainy, sunny, wind-blowing, or cloudy, cleansing day, feels the way it does. We can just walk outside in our day and say, "Wow— it just is! Isn't it a beautiful rainy, wind-blowing, cloudy, or sunny day?" Once we learn to detach, then growth will no longer have the biting effects it once had on our lives. We will be able to move through our growth with grace, peace and balance on all sides.

Embracing the darkness through surrender

One technique I like to use to embrace the acceptance of growth is by surrendering to the fact that growth is a natural part of the process in order for us to find the true inner happiness we've been looking for. By accepting and embracing the darkness as part of the natural process of growth, the biting edges of growth will cease to exist. There is one thing that's inevitable—we will never escape growth. By embracing the possibility that there's no separation between the dark and the light, the pain of growth will lessen.

I like to use the representation of the stars in the heavens as an example of the outer reflection of the inner existence of both the dark and the light as they coexist in unity as a total representation in the night sky. If there were only light when we looked up into the sky, we wouldn't even be aware of the existence of stars. Going through darkness is the process everyone must undergo in order to become aware of the existence of light. Without the existence of darkness inside of us, we wouldn't have the incentive to push through our self-inflicted pain and suffering that ultimately will lead us out into the light.

A key to going through the darkness with grace and lessened pain is through the acceptance of it as part of the never-ending natural process required to reach the light. Choosing to accept darkness as part of the process of reaching for the light will allow the growth process to become more manageable. This causes the darkness to transmute itself into a friend, instead of the enemy, or something to destroy and conquer.

Letting go of old stuck energy

Another form of surrender that can have a very powerful impact on growth involves realizing that growth is simply stuck energy that has to move out of the way in order for a new self-desired reality to come into existence. Think of the beginning of growth like a newly discovered dam in the river of consciousness that exists within you, where one day your consciousness became aware enough to see the dam and decided it wanted to break it down so that the water could flow through freely. As the dam begins to crack from the pressure building up behind it, caused from you and your inner contemplation and becoming aware of new perceptions, the water begins flowing down the river in a much larger capacity and puts more pressure on the old stuck rocks, twigs, roots and leaves embedded in its banks. In this way, it began causing the river to become wider, deeper and stronger.

Those sticks, rocks, or old things of the past, are equivalent to stuck energy or blocks and this process oftentimes doesn't feel very good as these things are being ripped out of their old foundation—kind of like an old, decayed tooth releasing its strong foothold along the banks and the bottom of its anchored existence along the entirety of the gums. We feel the pain when it is removed, because it is connected to the nerves and after it is removed, the pain begins to dissipate. The main thing here, is not to get caught up in trying to figure out what the sticks and the rocks are and how they got there in the first place. They've been there for a long time. It doesn't matter why they were there or how they got there; what matters is that they're on their way out.

I like to think of the process of letting go of old stuck energy as equivalent to turning on a light switch, where you flip the switch and the light turns on and illuminates the branches and rocks stuck in the river. Then, your consciousness becomes aware of them and chooses to eliminate them. It doesn't matter how the light turns on when the switch is flipped. The light just comes on. I personally don't see why it is necessary to waste so much energy dwelling on why those rocks and sticks from the past got there in the first place. I'd rather be rejoicing in the fact that they are leaving, that they no longer exist in my consciousness and can no longer hinder me or stop me from moving forward in my new chosen reality.

By holding onto or trying to analyze energetic-sucking forms of energy/mind chatter, one may experience their influences in ways such as depression, tiredness, lack of motivation and fear. This can even lead to undesirable physical manifestations in such forms as cancer, pains, rashes and many other forms of illnesses. This is another definition of the middleman. Cut out the middleman and you won't waste so much valuable energy. Growth is like a wave in the ocean. Sometimes it goes up and sometimes it goes down. The way we choose to ride the wave will determine the overall influence the wave will have over us.

Allowing for patience and love

Throughout this process, keep in mind the concepts of "loving allowance for all things in their own space and time, starting with yourself" and "there is no there to get to, where you are going next." We are immortal and that means we live forever and forever is a very long time. Remind yourself to be gentle, patient, loving and caring to yourself as you would be to a little baby, because no matter how old we are or how far we've progressed, there will always be a point in our lives where we are the little baby. Hold these words dear to your heart.

Finally, give love to yourself first and then to others. One cannot give from a cup that is empty, only from that which is full. Give to yourself first, until you are full, until your cup runs over—without judgment, without hate and without fear. Only then, will the unstoppable inner mighty river of love flow through you in its totality of purity.

From this river of love, you will begin to perceive that all drops of water make up the body of water; be it a river, a pond, a lake, a stream, or an entire ocean. All are an integral part of the Oneness.

CHAPTER 5

The facets of Oneness

The never-ending awareness of the internal facets in the Oneness are revealed to us through our experiences, as they expand themselves through our interactions with self and all life. I would like to start this chapter with the subject of space and time. By contemplating the possibility that space and time don't exist; we begin to release the restraints and the limits they both create to the possibility of the existence in the Oneness. I believe space and time do not exist and they only exist on the earthly plane. Time was created in order to solidify or bring something into order. Once we take into consideration that the only thing that exist is now and the concept there is no there to get to, where we are going to get to, next, then we begin to see time as an illusion. Take the life process of the rose for example. We can't force open petals on a rose, by adding a time restraint to when it's going to open. We could try, but as the lessons from the past have revealed, it causes the rose to feel invaded, lose integrity, lose its life force, look funny and do funny things it normally wouldn't do in its normal life process.

Take space, for example. If we take into consideration the perception of omnipresence, then new perceptions of omnipresence would seek us out and reveal themselves to us, because of the new resonance we've created inside of ourselves. By doing so, not only would we begin to realize things like planes, cars and trains are dinosaurs, but that space known as the distance between two objects, is truly an illusion. I have found that in order for me to anchor the reality of the Oneness into my consciousness, I had to begin by making a choice to completely let go of what I believed to be true, based on what I learned from the worldly perspective. By focusing only on the possibility that what is real such as, love, now, dissolving the illusion of separateness and making conscious decisions to stop holding things at arm's length, I began to experience the unique hidden facets leading to a fuller understanding of the Oneness. This caused me to contemplate in thoughts, such as: If there is only "one," this means that everything that exists and that has ever existed is within me—meaning the air I breathe, the substance that makes up the air and all things from the biggest to the smallest. For me, this was a very hard concept to wrap my brain around until I came to the realization that I couldn't find the Oneness with my brain. I had to become aware of all my senses and use them simultaneously to help me begin to see a glimpse of the Oneness.

One of the primary ways I like to get answers is through dreams, because dreams are another form of communication aside from our brain. So, one night before I went to bed, I asked my Higher Self (or what I like to refer it as my God-self), "Please show me something that will help me understand the Oneness, better."

When we ask our Higher Self to reveal something to us, the Higher Self will send us the best answer it has and sometimes that can come in the form of an angel, friend, circumstance, plant, symbol, or animal. So, keep a watchful eye, heart and feelings after such a request. As we move along in the process of dissolving the illusion of separateness and become more aware of the Oneness, we will begin to receive and discover many unique forms of communication that will be tailored to the enlightenment of an individual's unique process. This means that it's not going to be the same for everybody. That is the beauty of the creative process: it's creative!

Understanding the Oneness in everyday life

I had a dream where I was outside standing in front of a glass door leading into a large open room. In fact, the whole wall that the glass door was on, was also made of glass and I could see right through it; crystal clear. Then, all of a sudden, this large group of individuals came up from behind me and rushed past me. One person held the door open for the others as they proceeded to walk into the large room and begin playing with a large beach ball. They bounced it into the air and kept it up as each individual took turns hitting the ball up without allowing it to hit the ground.

As I was walking up to the door to go in and play ball, there was a person walking alongside of me. We stopped at the door and as I was waiting for him to open it for me, another person rapidly walked up from behind us and with his right hand, he touched the glass with his fingertips.

It was at that moment of contact with the glass when I noticed a violet light as it rapidly formed around his fingers and around the surface of his skin where his finger made contact with the glass. This light extended about a half an inch out from where the tip of his finger was touching the glass. He began to slowly push his hand through the glass.

As his hand was passing through the glass, everywhere the glass made contact with his skin, the violet light was present. I could see his hand all the way up to his elbow on the other side of the glass. Then he pulled his hand out. He turned his head and smiled at me and then to my amazement, he just walked right through the glass door. I said to the guy standing next to me, "Okay, how did he do that?" He replied by saying, "He was already on the other side." It was at this time that I began to see that he didn't actually walk through the glass at all. He just understood he was already on the other side because there was no distance between where he was and where he wanted to be. That was how he was able to do it: by being aware that he was all things and that nothing was separate from him.

After having this dream, new experiences of how the Oneness interacted in my life became apparent, such as in the reflection of my outward experiences and how they coincided with my inward realities. My outside experiences are really revealing the truth of my inner self. I can see now that my life is one big mirror. The interactions with others and circumstances that happen in my life aren't meant to be judged. They are meant to be seen as a mirror only to reflect my inner truth. Remember, if we change our inner truth, then shall our outer mirror be changed.

Finding answers in your employment circumstances

Oftentimes the work environment can become one of the easiest ways to get answers to complex questions. This is simply because of the sheer volume of individuals in your work environment and the bombardment of the reflections they present in forms such as their actions, interactions and words, just to name a few. Once we start viewing our environment and relationships as something not separate from us and choose to view them as the mirror, the magic begins to happen. When we allow the possibility of the reflection into the equation as a form of communication, it becomes hilariously easy to get answers.

For example, several years ago, I worked in a factory environment with approximately two hundred fifty people, all within extreme proximity of each other. I had a co-worker who later in the months to come, I gave him the nickname, Fortune Cookie. He asked me why I gave him that nickname and I said, "Because you give me the answers and you don't even know you're doing it. I just sit at my bench doing my work and asking myself questions and you'll walk right up to me and randomly speak two or three words completely out of context and it always ends up being the exact answer to my question!"

I told him, "You are the easiest reflection of me in this building." This revealed to me that this individual was a pure channel of divine inspiration! He didn't allow what other people thought about him to influence his actions. That made him an extremely powerful individual. Some people may have thought that some of the things he did were a little different, however, I thought he was one of the coolest people in there. He was very animated and what you saw, was what you got.

Watching him gave me a sense of freedom; he was telling me in his own way without words, "Be yourself, don't care what anyone else thinks about you and if you choose to do that, you will be the purest divine form you can possibly be." Oftentimes, during the week we would run down the hallways at work together while singing, "We're off to see the Wizard, the wonderful Wizard of Oz!" And other times, when there was a lot of stress in the air, we would just look at each other with a big smile on our faces and stick our hands up in the air shouting, "Wheeeeee!" like you would if you were on a roller coaster going downhill. We would be laughing all the way! The other thing I found that helped me see the reflection of the Oneness better, is when I became aware of the duality that the perceptions others were reflecting to me. Meaning, not only if I disagreed or agreed with their perception, but what was their perception reflecting to me on a personal level. After all, we wouldn't even be having our conversation, or interaction, if there weren't a reason connected to growth. The discovery that opinions had a dual purpose led me to be a better listener and not to have a kneejerk reaction any more, when I disagreed with somebody's opinion. Also, this led to me to be more understanding of other people's perceptions. I wanted to see the bigger picture, meaning the reflections, ripple effects of actions and the quality of love that was expressed through the diversity of our unique perceptions and opinions.

There are a lot of opinions in a work environment and as we all know, we can't change the opinions of others, unless they want to change. We can only give our opinions and try to meet in the middle to create a win-win situation. Sometimes it can be difficult to shift the perceptions in ourselves and in others in a way that creates positive ripple effects within our environment. Sometimes it takes time for changes to take place. As the old parable speaks, "Nothing happens before its season."

That doesn't mean to surrender or give up expressing your unique form of love, being expressed through your opinion. It just means as we are going through the process of change, have some fun with it. After all, we are dealing with a lot of different perceptions and as the rock band,

The Beatles, said, "There's nothing to get hung up about." As you've learned from previous chapters in this book, there are many ways to express love. The old forceful ways will cease to exist in the not-so-distant future, so we might as well have fun with it and stick our hands up in the air and just say, "Wheeeeee!"

The key to enlightenment is to lighten up

Of course, you can do the spiritual thing and just project love to the company and to the world and help shift the environment that way (wink, wink). But while you're doing this, you might as well have fun with it and not let that stuff bother you. The key to enlightenment is simply to lighten up. After all, don't forget: never were you the victim, but always the creator. That means there is some reason why you're here or there, experiencing what you are experiencing and being in that environment. You might as well put a big smile on your face and see it for what it is and not get caught up in the drama and get stuck and lose your energy, because that would mean that you are the victim, not the creator.

The Oneness is you!

Another way I view the Oneness is like this: let's say you're driving in a car and you think about something or ask a question. Then, all of a sudden, you have a feeling to turn on the radio in your car and as you do so, you instantly become aware that the song on the radio is answering your question. A car drives by and the license plate answers your question—or a sign on the road or passing animals or a plant. By integrating the Oneness, you can begin to realize that it is all you.

Another way we might look at it, for all of us brainiacs out there, is like this: instead of listening to your brain on the inside of your body, you are simply seeing an extension of it on the outside. To me, this tends to make me a lot smarter because I have expanded my brain to a much larger scale and am using more of it, so to speak. Not to worry, though; it won't make you look like you stuck your finger in a light socket, causing your hair to stand straight out! It's just another form of communication and realization.

When you see something on the outside of you that is blatantly recurring over and over again and giving you the answer to your questions through all of those seemingly miraculous coincidental circumstances, in forms such as the fortune cookie, radio, overheard conversations, license plates, billboards, numbers and so on, is really your consciousness speaking to you in the form of the Oneness. The discovery of these forms of communication have been made obvious through your intuition as it taunts you to gaze in their direction. It is not something separate from you. You are just becoming more aware of the extent of the Oneness.

Let me give you another example of this. One day, my wife and I were sitting in a restaurant and I was explaining to her this very concept of how the universe is constantly speaking to us, like a big megaphone shouting out the answers to all our questions. I was explaining to her that the more we get rid of certain chatters in the background of our consciousness, the more present we become and how that in turn will give us a stronger infusion into the Oneness.

I said, "Think of what you see around us like a big tarot deck. Just ask a question, turn your head and what you look at will be the answer. It's automatic. All you have to learn is how to trust yourself and how to interpret it like a dream by using another form of communication called symbols. Other times, it's just darn right blatant and you simply see or hear the answer. Our outward experience is really equivalent to our inward experiences and are no different than the dreams we have when we are asleep revealing to us their hidden secrets."

Then, after our conversation on this particular form of how I was becoming more aware of this form of the Oneness, it was time for me and my wife to leave the restaurant. As we began to walk out the door, I asked my wife a question. It was at this moment, in a restaurant filled with people, a waitress about five tables away from us, with the loudest voice in the room, spoke to a customer a seemingly random phrase and in doing so, she blurted out the exact answer to the question I had just asked my wife. And then my wife turned to me, looked at my face in amazement and said, "Wow, that waitress just answered your question!" As I stared calmly into her eyes with a slight grin on my face, I replied by saying, "Welcome to my world."

Here's another example. One time I was sitting on a bench next to a creek with my feet stretched out in a crossed position propped up onto a stone, just relaxing. Then, suddenly, a small gust of wind came up and a little leaf blew out from underneath the stone my feet were propped up on. I followed the path of the leaf and watched it all the way until it stopped and anchored itself on the ground. In my mind, I interpreted the leaf as a lizard running out from under the rock my feet were on. And then like a quick flash of light, I realized that the leaf was talking to me and telling me that a lizard was going to run out from underneath that rock. I turned my gaze back to the rock and stared at the area where I saw the leaf come out. All of a sudden, I saw the little head of a lizard popping out from underneath the rock and it ran in the exact same path the leaf chose and stopped actually right where the leaf landed.

Would you like another example? For two years, every time I drove past a certain stretch of road on Interstate 179 in Sedona, Arizona, I would always say to myself, "One day I'm going to go get my tomahawk." After two years of this happening over and over again, I decided I had enough and decided to pull off the side of the road and start walking in the direction where I thought my tomahawk was located. I started heading down a desert wash and then decided to walk up a small hill that was on its opposite side.

When I got up to the top of the wash, another thought came whisking into my mind. It said, "Look for the tallest tree and under there you will find several ancient artifacts."

So, I did what I heard inside of my head and focused my gaze across the top of the trees and saw one tree peeking out over the tops of all the other trees. As I started to walk toward the tallest tree and when I was about twenty yards away from it, my head suddenly turned as I became riveted like a magnet to a vertical cliff wall to the right of me. I was still, as I said out loud, "Any minute now, I expect some Indians to come down toward me from the base of this vertical cliff." Suddenly, I felt like I was walking through an invisible wall. In my best description, it felt equivalent to walking through a wall of gelatin; you could actually feel the viscosity of it. I realized I was walking through a wall of energy, as I felt it pass through my body until it was behind me. As soon as I was on the other side of the wall, I started hearing loud drums beating and people chanting. I just stood there for about five minutes, listening to the crystal-clear sounds the spirits who lived there were making. After the chanting and drum beating stopped, I started walking again toward the tree and began brushing the leaves from on top of the ground. I found five matates and five manos; stone tools used to grind corn and other items, buried in only three inches or so, of dirt. I then thanked the items I found using the words they spoke to me through their symbols and put them back exactly where I found them and camouflaged the ground so they would be safe. After walking around for hours. I began to get very tired and stopped walking and said to myself, "I guess I am not going to find my tomahawk." I gazed at the ground between my feet and noticed a rock buried there. I could only see a small amount of it exposed; about the size of a silver dollar and noticed a little groove in what I was seeing. I shouted out loud, "I finally found it! I found my tomahawk after all these years!"

Several months went by after this experience and one day I decided to tell a friend of mine about this spot. I gave her a verbal map of where to stop on the side of the road and I told her that I would make a round circle out of rocks and put a little arrow in it to point in which direction to go. I went to the spot and began preparing the marker. I started laying down my rocks in a circular fashion about one-foot round in diameter and began placing the three sticks in the configuration of an arrow; one long set of rocks down the center and two short sticks on the top of each side of the center one to form an arrow. As I was laying down the final stick to define one side of the arrow, an ant walked over, picked up the stick and walked away with it.

I said to myself, "Oh yeah!" and grabbed another stick and put it in the same place. The instant the second stick touched the ground, the ant in mirror image, dropped the stick that was in its mouth and turned around walked over to the one that I just set on the ground, picked it up and carried it off, too! I got really frustrated and said, "Oh yeah, let me see you take this one!" I got this huge (relative to the ant) round stick about an inch long and the thickness of my thumb and laid it on the ground in its place. And then it dawned on me that the ant was being possessed by a Native American spirit. I was told that it was okay if I went to that area, but it wasn't okay for me to show anybody else.

Then, that night, I had a dream. A Native American man and I were walking down the street on I-179 in Sedona AZ, hand-in-hand as he led me to find the sacred place under the tree and to my tomahawk. He walked me right to the base of the little hill that I stood on top of the previous day in order to be able to get a good vantage point to find the tallest tree and then he stopped, let go of my hand and left me there standing at its base. Then he walked up to the top of the hill and stood on top of it, as another Native American man came up from the backside of the little hill.

Both of them stood side-by-side for a little bit, looking down at me in the wash. They turned around and started walking back down the backside of the hill until I couldn't see them anymore. They started throwing rocks at me! I guess that was their way of telling me to stay out. I realized although I had permission to go there and was led to find my tomahawk, his friend didn't want me to show anybody else where they were. I spoke to them out loud using my third eye to see them and thanked them for showing me where my tomahawk was and told them I was sorry for not asking permission to show somebody else where they were living and that I respected their beliefs. After I spoke to them everything was okay. The lesson here is to always ask permission out of respect for others, their beliefs and the ripple effects our actions may create before we go trampling into sacred places and disrupting them. If we have permission, it's okay to proceed in love, integrity and respect. If we get a "No" after asking permission that means, "Don't do it." Meaning, don't give advice, energy and touch, or disrupt anything; let it be.

More lessons on Oneness

The reason why I am telling this story about the process of how I found my tomahawk, is because of the lessons I learned from it and how this experience was vital in leading me to grasp a better understanding of the Oneness and the coexistence of multiple dimensions, here on the planet Earth. Number one, it taught me that there are multiple dimensions that coexist simultaneously within our existence. We can't see them because they're on a different vibration, but they're there with people living in them and interacting just like us.

The second thing I learned through this experience is why sometimes we might see something unexplainable. I believe it is because oftentimes, depending upon our mood, we can shift our consciousness randomly, kind of like when you change the channel on a radio. Sometimes we accidentally shift our consciousness to the vibration or frequency that matches the one the spirits, angels, extraterrestrials and others, are on. Things that oftentimes can help change our frequency and go to the other channels, are rhythmic sounds such as drum beats, ringing bells, rattles and driving a car. We often get very clear messages when using these modalities as a tool.

The third thing I began to understand in regard to the Oneness, was that even though you may be looking at a bug, you never know who's working through it. So be careful what you step on—because, after all, you don't want to kill the messenger.

At the beginning of my discoveries of the Oneness, I started seeing license plates, signs, people, animals and plants answering my questions.

At first, I thought of them as a coincidence, but then I came to the understanding that it was simply just me speaking to myself through my outside experiences and their reflections, which led to the awareness that there is no such thing as a coincidence. Once I made this realization, I began to utilize an enforcement process by implementing these words every time I saw a sign or received some form of communication from the outside in. I would say, "That which I see, is not separate from me." By repeating these words to all situations and circumstances that I created in my life, not only did it enhance the magic, but it also completely eliminated without a trace, all existence of judgment.

As we begin the practice of receiving, giving and increasing communication with all living things, the sure act of repeating this phrase, "That which I see is not separate from me" can be a gateway to discovering the true meanings of inner Oneness, as it grows inside of you and reveals its new facets to the existence of Oneness, which will ultimately lead to dissolving the illusion of separateness. All of us can create the Oneness to abide in our consciousness.

CHAPTER 6

Creators, not victims

The reason why I decided to talk about this subject is because it is important to understand and integrate the idea that we are never the victim, but always the creator. This foundational truth will help us to become more responsible for our thoughts, actions and words, spoken loud from the inside and out.

Oftentimes, we just go through our normal days thinking and saying all kinds of negative things without having any idea of the repercussions they create, such as, "Why is it so hard for me to make money or get a job?" "Why do good things always happen for other people and not for me?" The secret is when something good or bad happens in our lives, it's always good to keep in mind, you are the creator. Bad things and bad luck happen to both good and bad people; there is no separation. The secret is in understanding why this is so.

Luck has nothing to do with it

I have found in my life the idea of back luck or good luck, never has anything to do with the circumstances or things I drew into my life. For me, the belief of good and bad luck was just a crutch. It was just a way for me to skate through my life, blaming everybody and everything else for all the bad things that happened and not taking the responsibility as a creator. After I made this inner discovery, by getting honest with myself, I began to realize I had the answer to my happiness inside of me, the whole time. The discovery was it was me that created my "good luck or bad luck." I began to realize it was my negative thought processes I expressed through my perceptions that created what happened to me.

When I began to make the connection that every time I thought or said something, it would happen, regardless of if it were good or bad. I then began to realize that the universe didn't know the difference between good or bad; right or wrong. It just did what I told it to do and it did so, with no judgment. This is because the universe is not separate from me. We are one and the same. Bad things don't happen to good people because a person deserved it or did something wrong or bad. It's just because the person didn't know that he or she was creating his or her own reality.

Oftentimes, this can be one of the most difficult concepts to embrace out of all the concepts that you'll ever integrate in your life. However, this is the one that has the most profound impact. In fact, one of the main reasons we have angels, is so that they'll catch our words and thoughts before they manifest. If you think this world is crazy now, it pales in comparison to what would be created if it weren't for the loving embrace of our angels.

Beware of what slips off the tongue in the heat of anger. The reason bad things happen to us in the first place is because God is all things: the dark, the light, left, right, up, down and unconditional—meaning that you get what you ask for, no questions asked. You can't run away from what you create. You can only create. So do it with your heart, eyes and ears open and you will create a much-desired result.

Our thoughts have the ability to create

One night, before I went to bed, I asked my angels to give me a dream to help me to understand (in a way that was down-to-earth) the reality that never in my entire life, was I ever the victim, but always the creator— that it was through my choices and perceptions, I did indeed, create my realities. I said to my angels, "I know one day when I'm teaching this, that somebody is going to ask, "Well, what about the little baby that something bad happens to? Do you mean to tell me that little baby created that?" I asked, "How am I going to answer this question?" So here is the dream they gave me:

In the dream, I was at a gas station filling up the tank in my car. After I filled up my gas tank, I went in to pay the gas station attendant. As I was standing there getting ready to pay for the gas, the cashier said, "Isn't this world a crazy place? You never know what anybody's going to do." I replied by saying, "I disagree. What if it were like this? See that woman standing over there at that gas pump right now, getting gas? She is no different from me, filling her tank up exactly the same way I did. The only difference is that inside of my head I was thinking, "I can't wait until I'm finished filling this tank up with gas. I sure would love to be home with my wife right now barbecuing some chicken, because I miss her and love her so much." However, inside of the woman's head she is saying, "I can't wait to get this gas and get out of here. I am so fed up with my husband constantly beating me. This is the last straw. I just wish somebody would come and blow my brains out and put me out of my misery."

Guess what happened next? There's a guy driving down the road in proximity to the woman getting gas. As he is driving by, because of human interconnectedness, he hears the woman calling him and says to himself, 'I'll do it—I'll be more than happy to.' Now mind you, this person kills people.

"That's what he does. He hasn't evolved yet to the higher understandings of love and is not even aware of its existence. In fact, here's a shocker— he thinks what he is doing *is* love! Therefore, he is doing nothing wrong; he is simply being himself. So, he walks right up to the woman, sticks a gun up to her head and blows her brains out."

I said to the cashier, "Maybe that's how it works. Since our thoughts have the ability to create (with no judgment) and are not separate from the Oneness, the statements the woman made in her mind were equivalent to getting on a telephone and making a command to the universe as it lovingly fulfilled her reality. At this point, one might ask, "Why didn't God step in and save this woman from being killed by this man?" This is because the thoughts and the actions were one and the same, meaning not separate from God; it would be like telling a tree, not to be a tree.

Consider this metaphor: leaves fall off trees and volcanos erupt. They are both just being themselves. If you don't want to get killed by the volcano, move away from it! It is up to you to be mindful of your thoughts and words spoken out loud. There is not a single soul on this planet who isn't an extremely powerful creator. God is unconditional love and not separate from any existence. God is the dark and the light, the good and the bad, the up and down, the left and right. Why would God look at his thumb and say, "I love my thumb, but I hate my thumbnail?"

What you focus on, is what you get

Whatever part of God you focus on is the part of God you get. Coming to this awareness taught me that in order to create the realities I wanted, I'd better learn how to change my mind on a dime. If I don't, I will keep re-creating the same negative realities over and over again. I figure if I am going to create my realities over and over again, I might as well do it with the realties I want to re-create!

For example, in 2009, my wife and I were in Cancun. We were at a beautiful pristine beach and when we looked out over the water, there wasn't a ripple on it. It looked like a sheet of glass. For some reason (I don't remember why now), I was really agitated about something. While I was walking down toward the water's edge, in my mind I was thinking, "I'm tired of being here and I just want to go home." As I was submerged in these negative thought processes, I began to hear in the background the faint voice of a little child. His voice began to get stronger and stronger as he was getting closer to me and it caused me to stop and turn around to look behind me. What I witnessed was the little boy rapidly following behind his father, walking toward the water's edge and kicking the sand out beneath his feet, throwing a real good temper tantrum. I began to hear clearly what the little boy was saying and noticed that everything suddenly began to feel extremely amplified, as the little boy said to his father, "I'm tired of being here, I don't like it here and I want to go home!"

It was at this time the father calmly turned his head back to his child and said, "Son, you can make this anything you want it to be. It's up to you." Then the father just turned his head back around, facing forward and kept walking toward the ocean. Of course, when I saw this, my first response was, "Wow, that was a total reflection of me or what!" That's equivalent to God speaking to me directly with no obstructions. It was at this moment I said to myself, "Yup, that's right; I can make this anything I want it to be. Nobody can do it for me—it's up to me and I just have to make a choice. I can either have a bad time here in Cancun and live in misery and pain inside of my mind, or I can choose to be happy." Then I thought, "Wow! I'm here in Cancun with my beautiful wife. Everybody's out having fun in the ocean swimming with their families loving one another and all I have to do is change my mind."

So, I raised my hands up over my head toward the sky and said out loud, "Wheeeeee! I am here in Cancun with my beautiful wife having fun. I love it here!" I then ran and jumped into the water. I shouted to my wife, "Honey, come on in, the water is wonderful!" At that moment, I learned I could change my mind on a dime and because I chose to do so, we had one of the greatest days of our lives!

Practice makes perfect

Here is another example. The other day I was watching the news. A mother was being interviewed about her daughter who had been abducted and they never found her. As I was listening to the mother, I felt deeply saddened, not only because the mother lost her beautiful precious daughter, but also because of the discussion she and her daughter had had right before she was abducted.

The mother said, "Three days before her daughter was abducted, she was telling her daughter to be careful when she went for walks, because a few years prior, a girl was abducted and they never found her. When I heard that, it made me even sadder, because I realized that this mother had no idea what she was creating. I'll bet from the day after she had that discussion with her mother, the daughter was constantly thinking, "I better be careful and be on the lookout, because somebody might abduct me like that other girl."

The reason I am telling this story is to inspire you to take it to heart and really watch what you think and especially, what you say out loud. I realize this is a new concept and hard to believe. We just need practice. We are so used to seeing, hearing and repeating negative sequences in our words and thoughts and by doing so, re-creating outcomes that can be undesirable.

All I ask is that you take some time to go back to a few times when something bad happened in your life. Take a good look and see if before those things happened, you weren't thinking or said something in reference to what you experienced. The Cancun story was how I proved it to myself and created a better reality with my words.

CHAPTER 7

How words create our reality

This chapter is primarily about the mechanics of how words can work in the background of our consciousness and how the connections of words oftentimes can create an undesirable manifestation of realities in our lives. Our perception of reality is the key factor in what guides our choices of words, actions and creations and the resulting ripple effects from what we create. This is why unique individual expressions are expressed, experienced and manifested here on Earth. I believe the old parable "You reap what you sow" comes from this very source.

We create habit-formed phrases based on experiences from the past and oftentimes, we just keep expressing these phrases over and over again, in everyday conversations, without even knowing why. Realizing these connections to our words exist and seeing how they are intertangled with our experiences and emotions from the past, is the gateway to one form of understanding and realizing how we create our realities. Acknowledging, seeing and integrating this reality leads us to the opportunity of self-realization, of never being the victim, but always the creator. This is what I believe Jesus meant when he said, "The *Word* is alive!"

One way I like to describe how words and their actions can alter one's environment, I think of words and the associations connected to them, as the main ingredient utilized in creating a genetic alteration for a certain breed of dog, or like splicing the branch of a lemon tree onto an orange tree. As we embed our realities and circumstances from the past into our words and mix them into our emotions, they begin to cause the dog to be molded into a unique breed and the fruit from the tree to develop the combined characteristics of both the lemon and the orange.

This leads to the automatic internalizing of their existence without even knowing why, which causes the path to their existence of being, to be on automatic pilot, leading to a unique formed reality, in this case, a fruit with the combined characteristics of the lemon and orange as one.

Once we begin to see the connection between the words we speak, their connections to our fears and the effects they have on the creation of our realities, we then can begin to realize if we don't become responsible and take charge in how we speak to ourselves and others, we will be trapped in an endless circle based on the past that can sometimes last for years and often for lifetimes. To realize that words and their emotions have a direct interconnection to the Oneness and that they call in the powers to support what we say and reflect on unconditionally, can be a key factor to break the repetitive cycle our words have created in our life experiences. The main thing that gets us stuck, is our collective fear to change and fear of taking responsibility for our creations and the ripple effect outcome.

That is why we have rules and regulations here on Earth that no longer work—because of our rigidity and fear to change. I call this, "living inside the box." When enough of us change the realities within ourselves to what we want to see coming to us from the outside, meaning things such as inner love, inner acceptance and inner peace, our sheer numbers will create a collective resonance and build up momentum as it changes the actions and reactions on the outside in a form called, *the reflection*. That's how we can change the world forever and bring heaven to earth. By seeing the value in taking the time to create inner balance, inner love and inner peace, we will be contributing to a combined effort in raising the vibration of the planet through the ripple effects of the Oneness. *"If we find the love within ourselves, the whole world will find it."*

How about this for consideration? Instead of buying and consuming a bunch of stuff that people are trying to sell you through trickery, because the sellers know that we are all trying to feel good, be happy, feel loved and ascertain inner peace, we understand and embrace, we already have the love, happiness, peace and balance, inside of us. This way, you can make a bunch of money if you want and use it to buy things you only need.

My point is this, think of this form of marketing the seller does, is like a drug dealer standing on the corner of the street trying to sell you love, peace and happiness in the form of a drug called, product. This causes us to extend ourselves in a never-ending perpetual motion of working hard to make money to buy things to make us happy and feel loved, as they convey in the commercials we watch on TV. Then, the drug they sold us wears off and we consume more stuff and this puts a big strain on our finances and well-being and planet earth, through over consumption of its resources, causing our beautiful planet earth to go out of balance to the point that she will decide to reboot herself and start all over again and then we will be wondering why?

How words can anchor into our consciousness

Let's look at how words can anchor and create a stronghold in our consciousness, causing us to believe, think and feel a certain way. Let's start from the day we are born. For example: Say you're a little baby and from the very beginning of your life your mom and dad start saying things like, "Isn't Bob cute? Bob, you're so wonderful! Bob, I love you! Bob, come here." The key here is to realize why you as the baby, believed your name is Bob. It is because your parents created this name and reinforced it by saying that name out loud repeatedly, until a synapse magically formed within the clear liquid substance surrounding the brain and began floating around until it found its resonance on the brain's surface and attached itself there.

It was at the moment of this attachment when you suddenly became Bob. In fact, you believe that your name is Bob so much, that if someone were to walk down a street and you had your back toward that person and he or she said, "Hi Fred, how are you?" you would probably look at that person like they had a big green bug on their nose. In fact, you probably wouldn't even respond to that person at all. This is because you believe that you are Bob so much, there is no way anybody could ever convince you otherwise. Understanding how we integrate our belief systems is the key to understanding how we can re-create them and make changes in our lives. In this scenario listed above, Bob's mom and dad were the primary element in Bob's life that determined his belief of his name. What if we had the ability to be our own mother and father and we decided to start from the beginning like a child and choose words to repeat over and over again until we believed in them and literally re-created our realities?

What if there were a way to starve unhealthy synapses (such as addictive, repetitive thought processes) that exist in our minds in such forms as, "I'm not good enough; I'm stupid, bad, ugly, or overweight," and so on? Doing so, we can completely re-create a desired reality way beyond our wildest dreams and imaginations.

Creating new word patterns

Once I came to the realization that our words have a major influence on how we believe who we are, I realized that I had to start searching deep inside of me to find the thought processes and connected word patterns that brought me sorrow, suffering and pain and then change them. So, of course, my next question was, "How can I find the word patterns that will bring me the desirable outcomes I want to create in my life?"

The answer I got was to get in touch with my feelings when I say certain phrases to myself. For example, if I said, "That was stupid of me." I would stop in my thought tracks and ask, "How does that make me feel when I say that to myself?" My answer might be, "Well, it makes me feel kind of crappy inside and depressed."

Then I would ask myself, "Well, what can I say to myself that would give me the opposite effect and create a happiness inside?" I thought, "Well, maybe I should just say I feel smart and repeat that over and over again until I believe it...because, after all, isn't 'smart' a feeling I'm trying to create inside of myself?" So, I did just that. I repeated over and over again, "I feel smart," all day long for one whole month until I believed it. And then one day, just as if somebody waved a magic wand over me, I woke up knowing I was smart.

Now, if somebody comes up to me and says, "I'm stupid," I just look at them in the eye and all I see is a big green bug on their nose instead of getting all triggered, believing them, giving them my energy and feeling angry. From the moment you believe what it is you have created, you'll believe it all the way through, down to your bones. And there is no way anybody can ever tell you anything different. That is how you know when you are completely healed.

After I was through with this exercise, I realized that I could have anything I wanted and all I had to do was to re-create the feelings I want to feel inside. So, after taking a hard look at my core feelings, I asked myself, "What are the feelings I truly want and would bring me the closest and the highest heavenly reality I can possibly create?" My answer was: I know all I have to do is repeat the words that best resonate with my true heart's desire. I asked my heart, "What do you truly want?" And my heart said, "Pristine inner Oneness, pristine inner love, pristine inner peace, pristine inner joy, pristine inner abundance, pristine inner balance and pristine inner health."

Once I came to know my truth of how I wanted to feel inside, I realized I just needed to systematically go down the line of what I wanted to create inside of myself and repeat the words over and over again, until I started to believe it. New synapses would form and anchor themselves deeply into my brain. I highly recommend that when you do the exercise below, you only do one affirmation at a time; the reason being is that we have multiple levels of consciousness that coexist within us and when we use affirmations, the old realities inside of us will feel like they're going to die.

Don't worry though, this is a sign you are getting closer to the end of the process. Please note some new realities may take a little longer than others to completely be changed. You will know which one it is by small fragments of the old reality bubbling up to the surface. When this happens, just repeat the best counter affirmation that fits, several times over, until the feeling dissipates.

Exercise: Forming new synapses

Repeat over and over again, "I feel pristine inner love. I feel pristine inner peace. I feel pristine inner joy. I feel pristine inner balance. I feel pristine inner abundance. I feel pristine inner health and I am pristine inner Oneness." I would highly recommend these however you can substitute the feelings you wish to create in your own life. Please remember to take one affirmation at a time and let it work its way through you.

Every time you feed your new synapse by repeating your desired word or phrase over and over again, the synapse begins to grow bigger as it anchors itself deep into the brain like the roots of a tree.

Starving the old synapses

Using these affirmations as a process by repeating words over and over again in order to re-create new realities, will oftentimes start bringing in thoughts and feelings of doubt and anger, such as, "This is stupid; this isn't going to work; this is hard."

The reason why these thoughts are coming in, is because of the life to death process of the old synapses. I like to think of synapse like separate living entities housed in your brain and because you are no longer supplying the old food they liked to eat in the form of old negative thoughts, speech patterns or thought processes, they begin feeling starved, shrinking and feeling like they are going to die. All of a sudden, one day a new synapse moves in next door formed by new repeated word patterns and this new synapse begins to get bigger and bigger until it's the size of Conan, because of all the food we give it. Pretty soon these other synapses are starting to look around and say, "Damn, where did that come from?" They also say, "Man, I'm really feeling hungry!

Nobody's feeding me anymore!" They start feeling like they're going to die. They will try their hardest to get you to revisit them in a last-ditch effort to keep themselves alive. They start crying out and begin acting up by saying things like, "This is stupid—why am I doing this? I'm wasting my time!" in order to get your attention, so they can convince you to start feeding them again.

When you start having these feelings, this is the time to amp it up and really reinforce your new belief system by repeating your new belief. For example, you may be repeating the words, "I am inner peace." Then one day, you may feel really bad like you're going to die. It is at this moment that the old synapse is getting ready to die and releases its bond from the brain. Keep hammering it with your affirmation until the old synapse magically disappears back into the nothingness. It emerges once again back into the clear water like substance (cerebrospinal-fluid) surrounding the brain, never to be seen again!

It is when this death process is complete, you will truly realize the impact the old synapse had in your consciousness by the feelings you will experience through its death process. This process can also be thought of in the same way as a withdrawal from using drugs. Then, all of a sudden, the next morning you wake up and you feel wonderful. That is what I call the *born-again* moment. You are literally reborn into a new reality, free from the past. You are now ready to expand your consciousness, beginning from your new anchored reality.

Living your new reality

The coolest thing about creating a new reality is that once you do it, you can never go back to the old one. You will truly know who you are because you consciously chose to re-create yourself and nobody can take that away from you. You will start from the point of this new anchored reality and grow in its existence. This can ultimately lead to a new awareness and new opportunities for greater and ever-expanding awareness.

As I said before, I recommend taking this process slow. You don't want to just go right down this list and try to get it all done as fast as possible, because of the deep connectedness to realities, feelings and other parts of your consciousness coexisting from the past, meaning, this life and past lives. It's a good idea to just let one work its way out in its own time frame, whatever form that may be. There are feelings and emotions that may come up when the big flashlight of this new awareness begins to shine into the darkness and tells all the other parts of yourself (the parts that still don't believe or aren't aware of these new realities) that it's time for them to leave now. That can feel scary to old belief systems. In fact, I would recommend that after you shift your reality, you give yourself at least a two-week break before you start announcing the next new reality to your consciousness.

You might ask yourself, "Why is it important for me to shift my realities and to find this inner happiness, after all, this is a lot of work and sometimes it doesn't feel really good?!" For me, the answer to that question was that I would rather not have to keep coming back to this planet thousands of lifetimes, working on the same issues and re-creating the same realities and things to happen in my life over and over again. I chose my parents, siblings, friends, relationships and situations that happened in my life. I chose them all, to challenge me and help me to see the reflection of my true inner self. Wouldn't it be cool to just make a choice to go ahead and try my best to do the work I came here to do, perhaps to the point where maybe this could be my last lifetime here? Or at least if it weren't my last lifetime, I would come back in a more pleasant, heavenly reality instead of a potentially chaotic one. I bet you can't guess which one I chose!

I believe that when Jesus went on his walk in the desert, was tested by Satan and said, "Get behind me Satan" he wasn't talking to a red being with big red horns on his head. He was talking to his negative thoughts that created what we have come to call, *hell*, because he realized the impact his thoughts and beliefs had on him. So, he told them to go away. Jesus knew how healing works in his reality.

CHAPTER 8

How healing works

We heal by giving permission to our Higher Self, meaning, the part of ourselves that knows it is God. We can use our angels, spirit guides or ET friends as a go-between to channel divine energies through our Crown chakra or the back of the neck chakra. The energies required to facilitate the maximum healing environment, is primarily through our hands, eyes and mouth. We can grow our abilities through taking action by doing things such as meditation, going to a healer to receive energetic adjustments and do certain body movements like, yoga and tai chi. Disciplined practice of these modalities can open and raise our energies, which will enable us to channel higher energetic frequencies. At the beginning of our spiritual development, our ability to channel higher levels of divine love and heavenly energies required for healing ourselves and then others, come in and flow through us equivalent to about the size of a garden hose.

By letting go of things from the past through modalities just mentioned we can begin to expand our energetic hose to the size of a large conduit allowing us to give and receive a greater flow of abundance in love. Once we open our energies to be able to channel larger quantities of love, our ability to see the hidden inner realities will be magnified our interactions with self and others, will drastically change along with the ripple effects and interactions. For example, one can walk into a room filled with people and just from his or her mere presence heal others just by looking at them. Inner addictions will drop away and we will begin to experience inner happiness. Love, joy, peace, abundance and balance will manifest way beyond our wildest dreams and imaginations. In fact, my angels told me that this is the greatest drug that ever existed.

I believe they are right, because this lasts forever and doesn't wear off in an hour or two, like drugs do.

The two primary healing chakras and how to use them

There are two primary chakras we use to bring in channeled healing energies. One is called the *Crown chakra*, which is on top of the head and the other is a chakra on the back of the neck, just a little below the area where the neck connects to the shoulders.

The Crown chakra on top of the head is primarily where high levels of divine love energies come through. This love can be magnified and used for yourself and others by using your mind's eye, meaning your imagination or third eye. Visualize a violet light coming out of your Crown chakra and see it expanding out to infinity looking like a funnel and then see a violet light filling the funnel, feeling like a great mighty river flowing down through your Crown chakra into your heart then down your arms to the palm chakras as it moves out through your hands and see this light encompassing what you're looking at. Keep the flow going. You can do this all in your mind's eye without physically stretching out your hands for people to see. You can also make a conscious decision to shoot the light out through your eyes which is a good added thing to do when you pray over your food or send it out the mouth, when talking to others and see the beams of violet light reach the person, surroundings or object, until you see a cocoon of light around the person or object. This can bring great healing to yourself and others and the cool thing about it is it will look to others look like you're doing nothing. The chakra on the back of the neck is primarily used for trance-type healings, where other forms of God (such as angels, surgeons and whomever is needed) come through to help in the healing process.

Regardless of what our belief systems are, there is not a single soul on this planet who doesn't utilize these two chakras along with all the other chakras in the body. We are all powerful healers, constantly channeling divine love. The neck chakra is more of a door way of sorts, a place where spirit can enter a healing practitioner/ person and use them as a go-between. The neck chakra is where master healers from the other side who could be billions of years old, angels, ETs, who are light years advanced beyond our technology, are allowed to enter the physical body with the healer's permission and facilitate profound healing.

Oftentimes, I am asked, "Why is it that somebody like Jesus, can do the miraculous healings he did and others can't? What is the difference between Jesus and us?" The only difference between a famous healer/ mystic and somebody just walking on the streets, is that the famous healer/mystic knows and understands that he or she is channeling this divine energy and embraces it, consciously interacts with it, trusts it and believes in the use of these divine forms of love.

It doesn't mean that the healer is special or has powers beyond anyone else. It just means that the healer chooses to embrace his or her connection to the universe and not hold it at arm's length. Anybody can choose to dissolve the illusion of separation and embrace the awareness of his or her true self at any given moment. Many people may be afraid to have other spirits come inside of them, but I assure you this, there is only one. That means there is divinity in all things and this includes everything that exists. We are the masters of our reality. In the context of the Bible, it says when a son or daughter asks their father for a fish, the father won't feed them a scorpion. Well, if that is true, then that means that God would never send us a scorpion. God only gives us fish. My point is this, if we trust God, then what do we have to be afraid of? God comes in many forms and has many mansions. We deserve our inheritance.

Healing through sound

Sound can be very powerful when used as an instrument to heal. I discovered this one day when I went out for a hike in Sedona, Arizona, to sort out some old inner turmoil. As I was sitting on a rock on top of a mountain, beside a tree, an urge boiling inside of me, encouraged me to speak these words out loud, "I give permission on all levels of my consciousness with no limitations to my Angels and guides and my higher self, meaning, 'my God-self,' to do whatever it takes to assist me in what it is I am here to create. Followed by it has been difficult for me to heal myself alone and have come here to ask for help and then I said, I am not feeling good inside and have tried everything I can to help heal myself, but I can't do it alone so I'm asking for your help. I give you permission to do whatever it takes to heal me from this issue, I am tired of it and choosing to let it go. So be it!"

Suddenly, this bird appears out of nowhere and lands on the tree beside me. I thought it was very peculiar that it was sitting so close to me and then suddenly the bird starts singing a beautiful melody. It sounded and felt magnified inside of my soul. My total being felt extremely focused on the bird's beautiful singing. I listened to the bird for about five minutes, but it felt like an hour. After the bird left, I felt so much better and then all at once a flood of knowingness came to me and I realized that the bird was channeling the healing energies I needed through the sounds it was making. I then felt extremely grateful and said, "Thank you!" to the bird and how grateful I was for what it gave to me. I then said a prayer for the bird for whatever it might need. After the seed from the experience of the bird was planted in me, I began to realize as the plant grew inside me, many other ways divinity uses sound to heal us without us even knowing.

These are some examples of how the universe uses our unique inherent talents to heal ourselves, each other and the world, through sound. Have you ever noticed that when you watch a concert everybody looks like they're in a trance? That's because at that moment they are in a trance-like state. Going to a concert or listening to music is the same thing as going to a healer. Singers are a strong force for channeling divine healing love. Hidden in the background they utilize their inherent universal connection to the Oneness and channel divine love through both their Crown chakra and neck chakra as it proceeds out to their fans through their mouth, hands and eyes.

Their fans receive these healing energies through their energy fields, such as their eyes, aura and chakras. As the tones intertwine through our energy fields they flow deep into our subconscious, revealing to us the hidden language of love, the Higher-self and angels, all coming from the Oneness. The frequencies that sound emit cause a shift in our consciousness by tuning our frequencies into higher states of awareness; kind of like when you change a radio station and suddenly you are aware of a new song or in this case, a new reality. The main purpose for these shifts is not only for us, but also for the ripple effects this creates through each one of us because of the Oneness.

Another way I like to compare the tones of the voice is that they are like a Tibetan chant or the sound of OM. In our unique way, we channel divine healing love as it intertwines through the tone of our spoken word or songs. Sound is a very powerful frequency that has the ability to pass through walls and travel very far distances, especially within our consciousness, through our inner connection to the Oneness. As the receiver of these energies, we plug into the Oneness and receive its embracing love. Oftentimes, unaware of its existence, it slowly begins to grow into our consciousness.

Healing through movies

Another way we receive healings is through watching movies or the television, as the directors, actors and participants are in cahoots with the universe and are channeling divine inspiration and awareness through their words, actions, sounds and symbolism. Some of these healings can trigger a release by revealing deep, dark secrets hidden inside our consciousness, from our past or present lives, or by bringing a mass energetic awareness to help shift the world to its next level of advancement. It begins to work in the background of our consciousness and ultimately shifts our realities like a great mighty wave, until the new awareness finely solidifies itself from our subconscious to our conscious. Before we know it, the world changes.

Although we may not agree on the content of some movies, if we choose to view a movie in the form of a possibility in receiving a healing message and not by the judging of it, we will allow the universe to share its love with us and create the opportunity to embrace its inner healing. Movies, series, cartoons, media and commercials, strictly from a feeling point of view, may look like entertainment on the surface and may even seem meaningless, but in the background of our psyche and spirit, they are extremely powerful tools to help shift the consciousness in the world. After all, in my opinion we wouldn't even be looking at what we are watching or wouldn't have gone to that seemingly bad movie if we hadn't been guided to go and be triggered by it to either reveal an inner secret or receive an attunement.

Healing through art forms

All forms of art are healing tools for the planet. As we raise our consciousness into the higher forms of love and awareness and work on our art form, we are literally channeling our level of consciousness and universal healing energies into the consciousness of the piece we are creating. That is why people can receive healings from an object, painting or sculpture, for example. Being aware that all things have a consciousness, is a major key into the effectiveness of our own creations. Being aware and believing that consciousness works through all things, means that nothing is an inanimate object and then we begin to realize the existence of Oneness, meaning that separateness does not exist.

As we raise our consciousness, the piece of art that we create also raises its consciousness, even if it's a thousand miles away from where it was created. Even if it's several years later into eternity (because don't forget, we live forever and forever is a very long time), the ripple effect is tremendous because the energies of the objects we create, will keep getting stronger, helping mankind and expanding energetically. We will continually receive the healing benefits of its creator forever. By being aware of our ability to channel and transfer energy, one can consciously make choices to do things with purpose.

For example: Let's say you're getting ready to paint the exterior and interior or a room in your house and you want to put a specialized energy in the paint before applying it. What I like to do is get all the paint and gather it into the center of the room. I extend my hands out in front of me and I visualize a violet light and pull it down through my crown chakra, located on the top of the head and bring it down through my heart and out through the palms of my hands. I visualize the light encompassing the gallons of paint. I use the color violet because I view it as the purest form of divine love because it doesn't have any definition. I found that once I try to add a definition to something on how it works, it puts what I'm trying to accomplish into a box, because my beliefs get in the way through their entanglement based on the past and the energies won't come out as strong or clear.

I then say out loud, "I create on all levels of my consciousness, with no limitations the healing energies that are necessary to bring in the highest levels of love, peace, joy and abundance beyond my wildest dreams and imaginations, for myself and for others, be put into this paint and when people come into my home, may they receive a healing and feel love, peace, joy and abundance. I create this on all levels of the consciousness with no limitations. So be it." Then, I paint the walls. Any modality or medium, regardless of what it is can be charged with healing energies that can be channeled through it to help you and others. The trick is to be aware that we are doing it; that's what makes it more purposeful and stronger.

Healing through the hands and eyes

Another form of healing is one devoted to the awareness of utilizing our hands and eyes as a way to transfer love's healing energies to others. This can be accomplished by visualizing a large funnel extending into infinite space of violet light with the tip of the funnel coming down through the crown chakra at the top center part of your head and going out your eyes or hands as a beam of violet light touches the person or object, you're directing it at. You then see a cocoon of violet light around the person or object being fed by the beam of light you are projecting, while at the same time using inner dialogue such as, "May you be in peace. I send love to you or I send to this soul whatever it needs." You can use your intuition to know what to send and if your intuition gives you no answer, I just say, "Please give them whatever their Higher Self wants for them. So be it." This technique can be very powerful in helping the planet raise its consciousness. The reason why I love this technique so much is because it looks like you're doing nothing, just walking into a room for example, but inside of you and through watching the outer reflection through the effect using this technique has on the person, can be quite illuminating. You can also transfer healing energy in forms such as patting others on the back, hugging them, or shaking their hand. There is never a time or a place that isn't in divine accordance. The people we meet and the situations we find ourselves in, are all in accordance to our chosen direction; it's not by accident.

Healing through the Oneness

We heal through the Oneness whether we believe it or not, because it simply exists and can't disappear. Through meditation and using other self-healing modalities, we will eventually eliminate enough realities that don't support the existence of the Oneness and knowingly, will merge with it. Let's just say, the existence of truth of the Oneness, has a way of creeping up on us. Healing through the awareness of the connection to the Oneness, makes any healing modality stronger because of the confidence of knowing you are truly onboard and working together as a team with the universe, not separate from it. You have and are using all its resources, such as the Higher Self, angels, guides, surgeons from the other side and ET's, at any given moment.

Due to the existence of the Oneness, we also are healing others from far distances because time and space don't really exist. We have omnipresence.

That means all the space you see in between you and a perceived object being separate from you, is you. That includes the little stuff, like energy, atoms and molecules. No matter where you stand, you are already there!

Another facet of how we heal from the Oneness, I learned from a dream. In the dream, I heard a voice shout out to me from the sky in the likeness of a mighty trumpet and it said, "Everything you do directly influences eighty people—think about that." I did so for many years, which led to the conclusion that everything those eighty people do must directly influence me. Which led me to the understand that we are also connected to their life experiences. This is how I learned about the existence of what I call, the soul group. The soul group individuals most likely are relatives from past lives or fragments of the same soul that manifest in physical from to help each other with difficult growth that is too much for one person to handle. We help each other in our growth simply because of the profound love we have for each other. How I discovered who some of these soul group people were in my life, was by noticing how every time I went through a certain issue, a friend would call me, out of the blue and is going through the same situation. Who are these people? These individuals are often family members, lifetime friends and those people who, when you first met them, you felt like you've known them all your life. This just goes to show how important each one of us is, to be here and that nothing happens by mistake, even if it seems bad. There is always a good growth reason. So, you see, you are being here in the school called planet Earth, means you are working on yourself. Not only is it worth it for you, but also for your soul group, the evolution of the planet and all its inhabitants.

When you go through with a healing process and enter into a new reality, you can watch the reflections around you to see what you have achieved by following their reflection your soul group will reveal to you. For example, one time immediately following one of these moments, when I was getting in the car to go to the super market, I saw a newborn carried by its mother. I also noticed throughout the whole trip to and inside the marketplace, that I saw at least five other newborns in several different scenarios. The awareness presented to me through the reflection of these little babies helped me to integrate the Oneness even more.

Healing through button-pushing and triggers

The term, *button-pushing,* normally occurs when two or more individuals are interacting or communicating with each other and something a person says or does triggers you or the other person, which oftentimes leads to both individuals triggering each other. Each person blames the other for how they made them feel. Button-pushing can be triggered by many things such as, the way a person looks at you, certain body gestures, patting you on the back or even something as simple as a hug.

For example: Let's say you're interacting with a person and you ask a simple question in a normal, using a relaxed tone of voice and because the person may have triggers pertaining to gender, they start speaking to you with tons of anger in their voice and treat you like a dog. You know you don't deserve to be treated like that and you are wondering why this is happening when a simple yes or no answer, would have sufficed just fine. The key at this point is not to get triggered along with them and create a huge bonfire of anger, by throwing more logs on the fire between both of you with knee jerk reactions. In order to accomplish this, one must be able to see the truth behind the turmoil and make a conscious decision to change their perception of what is going on and chose to utilize the opportunity given from universe, as a way to find hidden truths inside of oneself. If a person or action triggers you or makes you mad, it tells you more about you, then it does about them and vice versa. If we make a choice to use triggers as a tool, instead of choosing to play with them in the old ways, such as viewing them as a fault or he said, she said; I'm right, you're wrong; good, bad, etc., rather, we choose to learn from a place of nonjudgment. The growth process will become easier and faster. Used as a tool, triggers will accelerate the process of inner healing, because you will no longer be wasting time and energy on triggers. For me, getting through triggers and button-pushing didn't happen until I learned I had the power to change my perception of what was being triggered meant to me and I began using them as a tool guiding me to the light. It wasn't until I shifted my perception of triggers and started to see them as the universe literally yelling at me through my thoughts and feelings.

Like God standing on top of the biggest and highest mountain ringing a big bell; dong, dong, dong, with a gigantic megaphone, turned up to its highest volume, shouting out to me through my emotions and feelings saying, "You asked me for help and to show you why and how to bring in more love, be happier, have more peace, balance, joy, be a better lover and how to express love better, well, this is why you don't have these things you ask for inside of you." Many years ago, my angels came to me in a dream and told me, "When you're in your higher power, absolutely nothing will bother you." I thought to myself, "Wow! what a cool perception because it caused me to shift my reality to understand that button-pushing and triggers were my friend, not my enemy. They are an ally and a part of the journey to self-discovery and not separate from God." So, you see, triggers are a very powerful tool to guide us to the truth of what is hiding deep inside of our subconscious. After seeing the truth, then you can use many of the techniques listed in this book to heal them.

You are the creator of your own healing techniques

Oftentimes, people ask me what the best technique for healing is. I always reply, "The best technique for healing is the technique that you believe in." You are the creator of your own techniques. As long as you believe it works, it does. That's a constant in the universe. That means the angels and whatever energies are necessary in order to perform the healing, will work in accordance with how you believe your healing modality works.

My personal favorite healing modality is none whatsoever. I just believe that I am divinely connected to the Oneness and the universe's loving embrace pours out through me whenever it is necessary to heal myself and others. That way, my mind has a harder time getting in the way of the healing process taking place, which in turn, enhances the opportunities for miracles beyond my wildest dreams and imaginations to occur.

Learning healing techniques from others can be the first part of the learning process, which will eventually lead to self-discovery. I would recommend viewing learned healing modalities as just a guidepost or a map to get you to a certain distance, which will then reveal the unique healer you truly are. Eventually, through your intuition, new forms of healing will come through as you interact with the angels and heavenly realities. These new cocreated energetic healing forms will branch off and reveal new ones. Just like anything else, while you're growing and learning new things, each new growth and new lesson will then awaken an even newer never-ending awareness of realities and growth. There is no "there" to get to, next. Rather, there is an unlimited expansion of rooms for growth and greater understandings in all modalities of healing and in life.

New realities often come in forms of insights (as a little voice, or in our mind's eye in the form of a snapshot vision). These realities communicate to all levels of consciousness within us until all become aware of their existence, transmuting it into the *ah-ha* moment like the turning on of a light bulb. And then it becomes real.

The main thing is to trust what your intuition is telling you and believe in it. I like to use a Bible parable as a tool to help if any doubt begins to creep in. This is the one that says, "When the son asks his father for fish, he doesn't feed him a scorpion." To me, that means to trust and believe what you get as being real and under no circumstances, doubt it!

Belief is necessary for healing

I am often asked, "Why can some people receive miraculous healings and others not?" There are many answers to this question. One answer is that the person being healed doesn't believe that the person healing them can do it. Even in the Bible, when somebody came to Jesus and asked to be healed, Jesus replied by saying, "Do you believe that I can heal you?" If a person doesn't believe that he or she can be healed by a healer, it won't matter how tremendous or miraculous a healer is through the eyes of others. The person wanting to be healed isn't able to receive a healing and the person giving the healing isn't able to give it. The person simply isn't ready yet. Sometimes a person can have guard dogs inside of him or her, that don't allow healing energies to come through. This can be based on fears from the past or religious beliefs for example. The main thing is when receiving a healing from a healer, I like to be extremely open and have no preconceived thoughts based on my reality of what's going to happen, because I have found that it tells the universe that I don't trust it, like the parable in the Bible not trusting the universe to send me a fish.

I realized that my doubts and preconceived notions would water down my ability to receive my full intended healing. I realized that if I felt like going to a healer, it was because the universe put it in my awareness to do so. So, I just do it. As I was going through my own healing process, I discovered that I had lots of guard dogs. I thought, "What is it I have to do in order to get past these guard dogs, so I can finally set myself free?" I asked the angels to help me with this. And that night I had a dream.

In the dream, I was standing on top of an embankment looking down at a large waterfall. Standing along the base of the waterfall was a large group of people shouting up to me several times, "Ask the angels, ask the angels!" Then, in my next dream, the angels told me, "In order for us to be able to help, you have to give us permission." This revealed to me that angels, though they can do anything, can't help us with certain issues unless they have permission. This is because they honor our belief systems, timing and realities and will not intervene or manipulate our realities unless *we* give them permission.

But the key to remember in giving them permission is that there is absolutely nothing they can't do to help us. They can change our DNA or remove synapses in our brains and replace them with new ones that will better assist us in ascertaining a more heavenly reality. They can make adjustments in our energy fields and in our chakras—and that's just the tip of the iceberg. When working with the angels, I realized I had to just trust them and release myself from the bondage of worrying about how long their healing was going to take or if they did it. The reason being, is sometimes after they work on us, there is a releasing process our soul must go through before the new reality can take hold and exist in our consciousness. Sometimes things can happen instantly and sometimes not. The fastest way to slow things down when receiving a healing is, doubt, worry and preconceived notions, otherwise known as expectations. The fastest way I found for healing to take place is trust, believe and openness (no expectations). I think this would be a good time to share a dream I had right after I asked the angels to heal an issue that plagued me since childhood.

In the dream, I was walking through my house which, symbolically, means the mind and realized that somebody broke into my house and went into my closet (things I kept hidden in the closet) and broke into a large safe I had in there. The door on the safe was wide open (they took the things I had locked up in the safe and had hidden in the closet.) I had the feeling that I had been robbed and ran to the front of the house and looked out a big window and saw a clown with an old stagecoach (way back from the past) with a lot of old toys and stuff in it. As he was getting away (the clown represents a cartoonish personality running off with all my old childhood junk.) I woke up. I will say this, "The universe can be quite humorous in dreams and will oftentimes, remind us to lighten up and see the humor in things." Needless to say, after having that dream, I went through a cleansing for about two weeks; a disturbance in the force one might say. Humor got me through it and boy was it worth it when it was all said and done!

For some people, to help anchor in the belief in healing, a deep dive is necessary to get to the root cause of the problem.

CHAPTER 9

Diving in & cleansing

Diving into the darkness to find the light

First of all, what is darkness? I see darkness as anything that we hold onto that brings us sorrow, suppresses love, brings anger, doubt, shame and fear. We can find their hidden pathways deep in our subconscious by running toward our feelings. Many years ago, when I was going through some deep "shit" as they call it here on planet Earth, I was laying on my bed asking my angels, "What's the fastest way I can get through all the internal pain I'm feeling? Please help me, I will do whatever it takes. I'm tired of it!" So that night, I had a dream I was in a huge bathroom with extremely disgustingly dirty urinals on all four walls. Suddenly, this huge spinning funnel of shit opens up in the center of the floor. Its largest circumference extended to about two feet away from the urinals. As I was standing on the extreme edge of the funnel, trying not to fall in, suddenly Archangel Michael appeared standing on the edge with me and jumped right into the funnel of shit. He started to get sucked down into the funnel. He then looked at me and began waving me in and said, "Lance, come on in!" So, I jumped in and got sucked down the funnel and ended up in a basement full of shit. Along the walls were thin slits of space. When I peered through them, I could see a beautiful peaceful landscape. It made me feel a longing to be out there feeling the essence of its beauty through my entire being. After I woke up from the dream, I immediately realized, in order for me to get out of my shit in the fastest way possible and live my dreams, I had to dive into my shit and eventually would find my way outside again. All the while I felt steadfast that amongst all of the turmoil I was going to go through, Archangel Michael would be there by my side helping me get through it along the way.

The lesson I learned through this dream was priceless. It gave me the courage to move on because I knew I had all the help I needed and knew I had nothing to lose and nothing to be afraid of. I see it this way: I was born with my issues and chose my family because they were the best reflection of my true inner self. So why would I not do the work I came here to do? Was I going to die, then come back and do it all over again? I don't think so! I thought, why not just jump in and get it over with. So that way, when I move on to my next existence, I can receive the love I always deserved instead of keep living my life the old way from the past by creating addictions to make me feel better for a short period of time and then the drug wears off. That puts me right back where I started from not being able to receive the love I deserved, because old realities from the past wouldn't even let me see the love, even if I were hit over the head with the big two-by-four of love. By going through the darkness, we can truly transmute ourselves into the light and find the total freedom we seek or what we call the heavenly reality. They say freedom is the best drug that ever existed! If we choose not to go into the darkness, we will stay in a circle, recreating never-ending negative cycles. These cycles are the exact reason why we keep coming back to Earth, over and over again. Below is a channeled technique designed to help get us through certain types of darkness. I call it, *The String Technique*.

Exercise: The string technique

This is a technique I use to help me find old stuck patterns from the past and to help me get rid of them, so I'll no longer give my power away to them and help me to live more in the present. A good way to know when it is time to use this technique, for example, is when you are talking to someone and they say something or do something like a hand gesture, pats you on the back, winks at you (or anything that is a unique trigger for you) and you start going crazy inside.

What I do at this point, is as soon as I get the opportunity to be alone, I go and sit in my meditation chair or lay on my bed; any place that's just me and its nice and quiet. The reason why I like to go to a quiet place for this technique is because I want to be as focused as much as possible on this technique, so I won't be distracted by being in the heat of things with all my emotions flying all over the place. I will sit in a chair, take three deep breaths to feel relaxed.

I ask myself, "Why does this trigger me?" It is then, when a thread appears in the form of feelings or thoughts and sometimes images. As I begin to pull on the string, by following the increased intensity of my feelings, it starts revealing to me that I'm getting closer to its end, where it leads me to the discovery of something in my life that has brought me great sorrow, suffering, imbalance and pain.

I will know when I have found it, by comparing the feelings when I was triggered to what I found at the end of the string. I will literally, in my mind's eye, see myself talking to the person that triggered me and then line up side by side, both the triggered experience from the present and the experience I found at the end of the string from the past and compare the feelings side by side and see if they match. If both feelings are the same, then I know I found, *the truth*. The truth is what sets me free because every time I would use this technique, I would feel freer and freer, until I realized I could no longer blame other people for causing me to feel the way I did. It was my beliefs that I chose to hold onto from the past that were causing me to feel the way I did, not what was happening in my present interactions with others. Knowing the hidden truth of why and how we interact with others is extremely powerful and leads us to be the creator and not the victim.

Healing past-life triggers

In my endeavors of self-discovery in trying to figure out what made me tick, I stumbled upon a something I refer to as the, *Sniper in the Bush*. I call it this, because even after using all of my healing modalities and techniques, I couldn't find what it was inside of me that was creating the disturbance in the force; meaning the emotional turmoil. You can't see it, but you can certainly feel the repercussions of its existence in your consciousness. I discovered this when I used the string technique and kept pulling and pulling and found nothing at the end of the string to match my feelings. When I asked, "Why?" the answer I was told was, "Because this trigger came from a past life. It was at this time that I said, "Oh great! How can I heal that?"

The angels whispered in my ear and said, "Give us permission to help you." So, I did what the angels recommended. The only thing I experienced after giving them permission were some weird cleansing dreams and a few bad hair days, but after about two weeks, I felt wonderful. If at any time you feel like you're dealing with the, *Sniper in the Bush,* there are other ways you can get rid of this by pulling out the big guns and giving the angels permission to help. Remember angels can't help us unless we give them permission, because they honor and respect our belief systems. In fact, it is a universal law.

You might also go to a person who does past-life regressions. Having a past-life regression facilitated, is nothing to be afraid of. You will simply be assisted by a person who is able to take you into the past through a hypnotic procedure, in order to reframe your circumstance into a context that will allow you to release it. Then, like magic, the issue just disappears! I firmly believe that part of our journey here is to do the hard digging, so we can find the truth and after we find the truth, we are offered many modalities and opportunities to help set ourselves free. If a past-life regression resonates with you, this is the Quantum Healing Hypnosis Technique (QHHT®) practitioner who helped me: Barbara Becker. She is a certified hypnotherapist and does regression hypnosis in person and online. Her website is: www.barbarabeckerenergy.com

Exercise: Releasing past-life issues

If for some reason, you don't want to go through a past-life regression, here is another way I will ask the angels for help (and don't forget to give them permission on all levels of your consciousness). I will either sit in a chair or lay on a bed and place one hand on my solar plexus and the other on my heart. I then begin taking about five deep, slow breaths in the solar plexus area.

Then I say out loud, "I give my Higher-Self, angels, guides and whomever can help me, permission on all levels of my consciousness with no limitations, to assist me in doing whatever it takes to help me heal and release any of my past-life issues that are causing any chaotic disturbances pertaining to _____." (Here, speak the issue out loud, put some feelings and emotion behind it. Emotions and feelings are equivalent to the foot pressed on the gas pedal.) I then follow by saying, "…with no limitations—so be it!" For me, this form of asking for help has been most profound.

The reason why I often say the words "with no limitations" is because now, while I am asking for the healing, my consciousness is at a certain level of understanding of what I need to be healed from my issue. I may not even be aware of the greater ways that love can heal me and therefore, I am putting limitations on what I can receive in my healing experiences. When you use the words "with no limitations," the heavens will open up to you in ways never dreamed of.

The deeper realities of healing

I think this is a good time to discuss some of the deeper realities of how healing can work in the background of our consciousness. As I stated before, we are multidimensional beings with multiple levels of consciousness coexisting simultaneously, interacting and combined as one. In order to totally heal ourselves, the healing must be done on all levels of our consciousness, in order for it to take hold. Once the healing takes hold, it's done forever.

I like to use the example of the process of how the continents were created, to give a visual of what I mean when I say, once we make a transition, we can't go back. At one-time Earth's continents were all together, scattered in large clumps across the surface of our planet. As

Earth evolved through its polar shifts, causing the expansion processes to begin, the continents split apart and created separate continents, which caused the Earth to expand into a new reality.

As you can see, those continents will never be able to be put back together the same way they were before—and neither will we. We will just keep expanding. Often as we expand our consciousness, things can get a little bumpy, as you can imagine how those continents were, when they were going through their transitions. I like to call the process when the small remnants of an issue are coming up and out to the surface, as tiny bubbles popping up in the form of emotions and chaotic thought forms. It is at this time I like to use humor as my main tool and keep repeating over and over again that song called, *Tiny Bubbles*. Doing this, allows me to lighten up a little. It allows me an opportunity to choose to love myself and view myself as a little kid just trying to learn how to tie his or her shoes for the first time and not beat myself up because I am not making a mistake or have done something wrong. I am just learning and growing and that's all.

Remember, there's not anything wrong with how you're releasing it or doing it. Just accept it as part of the process. Remember when the continents were separating from one another? I'm sure they weren't saying to themselves, "I hope I'm doing this the right way!" You can't run and hide from growth, so you might as well have fun with it. Sometimes I like to stick my hands up in the air similar to the way I would on a roller coaster and say, "Wheeeeee!"

When you have tiny bubbles, that's just letting you know that you haven't been completely healed on all levels of your consciousness yet and that your issue is still working its way out. You will know when you're completely healed of an issue by testing yourself. If you use your imagination and put yourself in the circumstance where your core issue used to exist, it will feel like you have amnesia—you can't find it, no matter how hard you look. That's when you know you're completely done and you will no longer feel the bondage from the issue, through its pull or emotional turmoil and its chaotic existence. I believe that by utilizing this technique, one can even eliminate bipolar characteristics.

Going through the process of healing

Most of the time when people find out that they can change their reality into anything they want, they move too fast without being aware of certain things. For example, we are literally billions of years old and have lived several lifetimes here on the school called planet Earth. These lifetimes are coexisting simultaneously and when you ask for something to be healed, the ripple effect touches all of those realities because of our interconnectedness. Oftentimes, when we ask for these adjustments, mysterious symptoms can appear and disappear, sometimes quickly and other times a little longer.

These symptoms can occur as rashes, pains, or emotional turmoil. A lot of times people will even go to the doctor saying, "I have this pain or this rash," and the doctors can't find out what's wrong. That's because it's on an energetic level and can be connected to a past life traumatic experience. Sometimes you can experience certain things that will only last for three days and then all of a sudden it disappears in the same fashion in which it came. Normally, these circumstances will occur the very next day after you have adjustments from the angels or do a ceremony. You can also have disturbing dreams that make you feel unsettled when you wake up. These dreams are cleansing dreams and this is simply a part of the letting go process. Try not to be afraid of them, rather, just be aware of them. When you have these disturbances from doing a cleansing, I recommend detaching. Don't add gas to the fire by trying to decipher it from belief systems based on where you are at the moment, for this may add negative influence and make the releasing process a lot harder than it needs to be.

I choose to view these disturbances as a tool that is revealing to me that I had the adjustment and that I am on my way to freedom. The other option is to make a mountain out of a molehill by saying things like,

"I'm tired of this; I thought I was done with that!" I highly recommend the first route; just surrender. Everybody on this planet experiences these forms of releasing. The key is to embrace it, love it and thank it for what it is revealing to you.

I guarantee that these cleansing processes (although sometimes they may seem to be a little uncomfortable) are worth it, because what you're actually feeling is the truth as it leaves the inside of your consciousness, revealing what was hidden deep inside your subconscious, all along. And like they say, better out than in.

Go slowly when releasing

Again, please go slowly when you ask and give permission to the angels to help you in releasing things. Also, remember that when we asked the angels to give us adjustments to raise our consciousness in ways such as asking to be more psychic or aware, or to open our chakras, it can result in physical repercussions such as monstrous rashes and pains in the body. Oftentimes, when we find out that we can create anything we want, we may do something like have a ceremony on top of a mountain and shout out at the top of our lungs, "I am now the most powerful healer who ever existed on the planet and all of my issues no longer exist. So be it!" And then all at once, all of who you were from the past including its old belief systems that are still connected to you physically and emotionally, must make the shift. That would be like not believing in ETs and then one morning you go into the kitchen to get a glass of milk and there's an ET asking you, "What's up?" That would be very shocking to your system.

If we choose not to take into consideration the existence in the background of coexisting realities in our consciousness, we may accidentally start going too fast. Rapid acceleration in the healing process often will result in feeling very chaotic. When utilizing any self-healing technique, I recommend only working on one issue at a time until you get use to what the process of releasing feels like. Become its friend by accepting the cleansing as part of the process to elevate happiness. After releasing a few issues, you will become and feel stronger and might be able to take a little more on at a time. If, at any time, the cleansing begins to feel unbearable it's time to take a break from any type of healing work and do absolutely nothing. Doing this work is very hard work. It's not a pill. It's lasts forever. So please, wait until the waves calm down. It's important to give yourself a little break; otherwise, you may create a very chaotic life.

Also, please take into consideration for if some reason you want to "Rambo" it and go as fast as you can, we don't have to do everything in this lifetime. Taking a break is a form of Self-love. It gives us some time to recuperate; after all, remember, there's no "there" to get to, where you've got to get to next. We are all immortal. That means we live forever and forever is a very long time.

Definition of the cleansing process

I like to think of cleansing as the death process of an undesirable fragment or belief dwelling within the soul. Realizing, that at the moment of releasing or letting go of an undesirable reality, we are literally feeling like we are going through an internal death, because of the feelings our soul fragments are connected to and the realities they represent within our subconscious. For example, let's say for thirty years through the process of introspection, our soul discovers a fragment of reality that doesn't allow it to experience the higher levels of love, happiness and abundance. All of the sudden, the soul realizes that in order to have what it wants, it has to change its reality and evolve in order to get what it wants. This may happen by using some of the techniques in this book in order to create the happiness you desire. Think about how that old part of the soul feels when it's told it can't believe in the same way it used to believe and all of a sudden, the old part of the soul realizes it has to work hard in order to change. Plus, the shock it feels when it realizes that the old belief was just fairy dust to begin with. It's like when you tell a loved one that they shouldn't take drugs because it can ruin their life and they fight you tooth and nail to try to prove you are wrong. These are the same feelings we experience when we are going through the cleansing process; like withdrawal from addictive substances, if you will. One really cool thing I discovered about the cleansing process is that when using the techniques in this book and you're feeling really bad because of the cleansing, you can use these feelings as a tool or a guide to let you know when you are getting really close to achieving your new desired reality. Just focus strongly on the modality you are using, to shift your reality to the new one and surrender to the pain of cleansing, so you can ride the wave onto the shore. Once you make it to the shore, that is what I call the born-again moment, or "I was blind, but now I see." Also, remember the cleansing process or the darkness as some may call it, are our allies. This goes hand and hand with the process of leading us to the light. When going through the cleansing process accept and surrender to it, like a glass allows itself being filled with water. Allowing the process to occur, is equivalent to riding the wave to the shore on a surfboard. It's best not to beat yourself up and fight it with thoughts such as, "This, sucks!" and "When am I going to get it? How much longer is this going to take?!" When you do this, it is equivalent to falling off the surfboard and getting churned up by the wave leading to the shore. Both ways get you to the shore. One is just more graceful than the other, that's all. It's your choice.

The art of cleansing

Cleansing is an important part of our soul's growth. Simply because it derives from the predecessor of unpleasant realities still present in our consciousness, as if they are still happening in the present time. As these old belief systems from the past are leaving our consciousness, they can often possess a vast ripple effect to our state of being, through our feelings and emotions. The word that best defines this process is, cleansing.

Cleansing can be quite a challenge at times only because of our perceptions of what cleansing means to us as individuals. Cleansing normally accrues when we perform self-healing, go to a healer or do a ceremony for releasing old stuck energies. Asking for an adjustment for the purpose of raising our consciousness can ultimately lead to afterward feeling kind of yucky, sad and confused. By experiencing the cleansing process, eventually it leads to anchoring the belief of a new perception in your consciousness and once your new chosen reality takes hold, it has the tendency to begin to run on auto pilot. Meaning, after you learn to ride the wave to the shore using the surfboard, you will become an expert at it and you will feel a slight twinge of an effect somewhere in the background of your consciousness or as some may say, a slight disturbance in the force.

Tourniquet to ease cleansing

This is the technique I use when I am going through heavy cleansing and just need some relief while the old energy is leaving. I either sit in a chair or lay down in a bed and I say, either silently or out loud, "I call on my Higher Self, angels, guides, star-born ancestors, or anybody who can help me and I give you permission, on all levels of my consciousness, with no limitations, to do whatever it takes to help me feel better. So be it." Then, I put one hand on my solar plexuses and the other on my heart, deep breathing and concentrate on my breath flowing to the spine. I totally surrender to the energy without any preconceived notions of what's going to take place. The reason I choose to use the words, "I give you permission on all levels of my consciousness with no limitations to do whatever it takes to help me," is so I don't reduce the quality of healing energy I receive or dilute it by putting it in a box based on my perceptions of where my awareness is pointing, at the time of asking for help. There are additional tools for clearing, cleansing and healing. One tool I have found profoundly helpful are stones.

CHAPTER 10

How stones heal

Throughout ancient times, our ancestors used stones for their unique energetic frequencies and the knowledge each stone contains. Oftentimes, I'm asked, "How do stones heal?" Stones heal because they have a consciousness; in other words, they are alive. Even in the Bible, Jesus said, "If I told people to stop clapping and praising my name, the very rocks would do it."

After reading this parable you might ask yourself, "How could a rock clap and praise a person's name if it isn't alive and doesn't have a consciousness?" Think of a stone like an individual person. Each person resonates on his or her own energetic frequency with a unique amount of knowledge ascertained from his or her life experiences. Just like us, when we are looking for a healer to help us through our life processes, we seek out the person who best resonates with us because of the energetic frequency that person holds. That's how we do it with stones, too. There are certain stones that we gravitate to, that hold a unique energetic frequency that can help us raise our consciousness to new levels of awareness. Basically, in a nutshell, as we go through the process of raising our consciousness, one day we discover that in order to raise to a higher level of awareness, we need help.

Our Higher Self calls out to the universe and asks from infinite aspects of itself for the answer to a particular question pertaining to healing and then the universe chooses a facet of itself, in this case a stone, to help facilitate the healing. For me, when I ask for a healing from my Higher Self and the answer I get, is to use a stone of some kind, I get a feeling inside to want to go on a hike, to a craft show, or to a metaphysical store. I get drawn like a magnet to a specific stone, pendant or necklace needed to facilitate the healing. For example, we may go into a store and have a strong attraction to a particular stone or somebody may come and hand us a stone, or we may be attracted to a stone lying on the ground or go to a craft show and be attracted to some kind of jewelry that has a certain type of stone in it. The main thing is to be open-minded. Love and healing come to us in many forms.

Stones are alive

The other thing that's cool about stones is that because they are alive and have an awareness and a consciousness, so they can receive programs, which is equivalent to an adjustment humans receive. In fact, shamans oftentimes will enhance many types of objects by changing the molecular structure of an object by using energy and channeling it into objects, such as staffs, clothing, liquids and many others. This is done to help a person to obtain the specific energies needed for their healing.

One thing a shaman might do, is to get a small cloth and enhance it with protection energy so that they can wrap the crystals they use for healing into it so that no outside influences can attach themselves to their crystals. In fact, crystals are extremely sensitive to energetic interactions, meaning that if you have a special crystal that you use for healing, it is oftentimes not a good idea to let other people look at it or touch it unless you know the person really well and allow him or her to do so, because of that person's integrity. In fact, you can go on *YouTube* and type in," human emotions affect water" and watch a video on water viewed through a microscope and see the different crystal formations created after the words love, peace and gratitude were added to it. Well, the same thing that happens to water, happens to all objects because all objects are a form of energy and have atoms and molecules that can be altered when exposed to a form of energy.

Exercise: Clearing stones and crystals

There are many techniques used for clearing stones. The one I like to use is to is just to hold the stone or crystal between your hands in front of your heart in a prayer position and bring the violet light down through your Crown chakra, that's on top of your head and visualize it going down through your core, through and out your heart and palm chakras, all at once into the crystal. Resembling a river of violet water pouring into your head and flowing out through the three chakra points, into the crystal and say out loud, "I open this crystal and create that any outside energies that are not align to the purest form of divine love and isn't aligned with what my Higher Self has created this crystal to do, be wrapped in love, released and be absorbed by Mother Earth. And that this crystal only works and heals in its purest form with no limitations— so be it." And then say out loud, "I now close this crystal."

Selenite: the healing stone

The best way I know how to program a crystal or any other stone for that matter is by utilizing a stone called, selenite. When you first get a piece of selenite, I highly recommend that you do a cleansing on it because you never know who touched it before you got it and what kind of energy that person or persons had. You are also going to use this special selenite for programing. I recommend keeping the stone out of reach of others, meaning, don't let anyone touch it or look at it because of the fact that we give and release energy through are hands, eyes and mouth. You can cleanse your selenite by using the same process used on "cleansing stones and crystals." To program your crystals and other stones using selenite, what I do is I put the stone to be programmed in my left hand with my hand opened and my palm facing up. Then clenching the selenite in my right hand, I point it towards the crystal being programed about three inches away from it and rotate my hand in a clockwise circle three times and then extend my hand straight up pointing selenite to the sky and visioning a vortex looking like a tornado spiraling out to infinity, then bring the selenite back down and point it to the crystal then visualizing a violet light coming down through the eye of the funnel into the crystal. While keeping the selenite pointed at the crystal, I also like to bring the violet light down through my Crown chakra and down to my Heart chakra. Then take the violet light down my right arm and out my palm chakra through and out the selenite while feeling and visualizing the violet light as it's coming out of the selenite and going into the crystal. I then say out loud, "I open this crystal and choose to program it with the purest form of love energies and frequencies needed to assist me in my abilities to help heal others and create that only the purest forms of divine love can be channeled through this crystal with no limitations. So be it!"

I just hold the selenite pointed to the crystal until my intuition says I am done. When I feel the programming is complete, I close by saying, "I now close this crystal. So be it." This is just the words I like to use to program crystals and can be used as a guideline for you. You don't have to program your crystals using exactly the same words I do. You can use many variations of words that best fit you. After all, you are the creator and have unique perceptions and reasons for what you want to use your crystal for. I recommend programing your crystals to what best suits your unique purpose. The main thing is to believe in your way of programing your crystal. If you believe it, then the universe will believe it and will conspire to do exactly what you said your crystal is intended to do, in order to help you accomplish your desired outcomes. Also, as you're going through your healing process and your Higher Self, a dream, or a psychic recommends a certain stone for you and you want to find the deeper meaning of a stone, the book I use and recommend is called, *Love is in the Earth, by Melody*. I personally like to use this book as a tool. I believe that if I have a dream of a stone, it not only reveals the stone I need to help me progress in my healing, but that it also has a double meaning as a map of sorts to reveal through the description of a stone's meaning, what direction my soul is pointed and reveals what I need to do next to progress my soul.

Selenite for meditation

Selenite is an excellent stone when used for meditation because of its very high frequency. When using selenite for meditation, I recommend placing the stone in your left hand with your hand opened and your palm facing up. The reason why I like to hold the selenite in my left hand when meditating, even though we can give and receive healing energy to and from sources of energy through both hands simultaneously, is because the left hand is on the feminine side of the body and is primarily used for receiving energy and the right hand is considered the masculine side and is for giving energy. One way that helped me to get a better picture of how the feminine side verses masculine side functions, pertaining to one side being the receiving side and the other for giving, was to compare the two sides as equivalent to what we would perceive as biological gender and their sexual functions. The male gives his seed to her and the female receives his seed.

Meditation with selenite

Sit in a chair and place the selenite in your left hand then visualize a violet light coming down through your Crown chakra, going down and through your whole body. Then, see your body get big, so big, that you see yourself as a giant, floating in space and you can see planet Earth below you. Then, visualize a cocoon of violet light around you being fed by the beam of violet light coming down from above, like an umbilical cord connected to the cocoon that encompasses you. Now move your focus to the selenite and feel the violet light passing through the selenite, through your palm chakra and feel it going up your left arm and allow the feeling of the violet light to fill your whole body as you're sitting in your chair, deep breathing through only your solar plex area. Stay really focused and surrender to the feeling of the energy and your deep breathing. Allow them both to consume you. After about twenty minutes, slowly bring your focus back into the room and slowly open your eyes.

I highly recommend that all forms of meditations be done for no less than twenty minutes a day and that they be done every day. Find a favorite spot to do your meditation, so you can build up energy there. Meditation is very sacred, so if all possible, I recommend doing it in the same place every time and if for any reason you can't do that, then at least clear the energy of the area where you meditate.

How to create a vortex for meditation

Creating a vortex on either side of a wall, behind or under the place where you do your meditation, can be very powerful. It allows your angels, guides, energies and others you may be in communication with, an easy access to a chosen location. Think of it like an open door, so to speak, between the two realms. Before you create a vortex, you may want to take some time and think about what specifically you want your vortex to do. Think of it in the same way you would program a crystal. I recommend when making a vortex that you create it to have a specialized function. For example, if you're creating a vortex specifically for meditation and self-healing, this is the procedure I would use:

Mindfully pick the location you would like to create your vortex. Then, with your right hand rotate your hand close to the place you want to create it in a clock wise direction three times and each time making the circle larger while extending your arm out. In your mind's eye, make it look like a funnel. Then with both of your hands extended out in front of you, pointing to the location of the vortex, say out loud, "I am choosing to open a vortex here in order to enhance my meditations, to create an easy access for the universe to communicate to me. I create that only my angels, guides, star born ancestors and the purest form of love and healing energy be able to come through this vortex to help heal me and guide me. I create that at this time that this is the only thing this vortex is used for unless my Higher Self wants to make a change for my greater good or the greater good of others. So be it." Of course, you can add anything you want when creating a vortex and fine tune it when you become aware of new perceptions and realities and give more depth to the interpretation of your dreams.

CHAPTER 11

Dreams and their significance

I believe that there is no such thing as an insignificant dream. People will often say to me, "I think dreams are just coming from experiences and things that happen to us throughout the day and we're just releasing stress. In fact, I had this dream last night, but it was so insignificant that I don't feel like it's even worth mentioning." I reply by saying, "Oh, then that means it's probably one of the most important dreams you've had this year!" Then they proceed to tell me their dream by saying, for example, "Last night I was watching a documentary on dolphins and all night long I was having dreams about dolphins. So how would you view this?"

My answer to this question is this: "If I had two viewings of dolphins in such proximity, it would reveal to me that the universe is trying to show me something that is extremely important, because the universe revealed it to me twice, once during the day and again in my dream, in order to get my attention and show me how important it is to get its message and decipher it. The universe oftentimes uses repetitive methods in order to grab our attention, for example: a shirt with dolphins on it, a catalog cover with a dolphin on it, radio personalities talking about dolphins, a bumper sticker with dolphins on it, all happening in the same day and oftentimes, within minutes of each other. Trying to make it obvious like a big bell ringing inside of you, saying, "Dong, dong, dong—look at me, I am important!"

After realizing synchronicities from communication from the universe and repeatedly using them as guidance, you will begin to integrate this form of communication as part of your daily reality, like a new language.

That's when the magic starts to happen and getting answers from the universe becomes extremely easy.

The different facets of dreams

Due to my experiences with dreams, I put a strong emphasis on how they can be one of the primary factors in our personal healing process, as they oftentimes reveal to us the truth of the current direction our souls are pointing. They can also give us a heads up to let us know when to expect the beginning of a cleansing, reveal to us what we're cleansing, where we are in the moment of our spiritual development and give us a slight insight to where we're going in the future if we stay on our current path. Through the years I have realized that there are at least three types of dreams. The symbolic dream, the soul traveling dream and the visitation dream.

The power of symbols

It's important to understand symbology. Symbols have been used by healers and associated in the process of healing the planet for thousands of years. I like to think of it like this: symbols are what energy looks like in its physical form. By implementing living energetic symbols on the Earth, on a person, or even wearing it on a piece of jewelry, this is equivalent to looking into the face of God or shining a flashlight into the darkest areas of our awareness, as we are being blasted with love coming in its purest form. This is because symbols have no earthly definition and can't be put in a box to dilute their purity. As our consciousness is fastened upon the symbol's existence, we are collectively receiving its healing effects as it ripples through us all in its loving embrace through our connection to the Oneness.

Take the crop circles, for example. I believe the symbols that are produced in crop circles are actually activations. I like to think of them like Reiki symbols. When these symbols are utilized, they literally have a frequency that causes energies to awaken and move to reveal the existence of new realities.

The planet is alive and interconnected as part of the Oneness, so when symbols (in this case in the form of crop circles) are created on the planet, it literally causes the planet to shift into a new state of consciousness, as the ripple effect of the symbol's frequency influences not only Mother Earth, but also us, because we are connected to her. That's why I believe we're going through some of the things we're going through on earth at this time. Love is ferreting out old negative belief systems. When old belief systems have to leave because a new form of love, frequency is ushering them out to take their place, it doesn't feel very good because of their connection to our old belief systems and their tentacles connected to our emotions, coexisting lives and even past lives. Even Mother Earth gets a little grumpy by her rumbling, blowing winds, heavy rains, volcanoes erupting and many other unforeseen types of chaos. Which in turn, causes us human beings to make shifts to higher levels of love, by teaching us what is more important in life, like giving and receiving more love, helping others, compassion for others and even breaking the barrier of race. This is all done through the cleansing turbulence of Mother Earth in the form of destroying the objects we were taught by the worldly perspective to be more important and of higher value.

Symbolic dreams

Even though symbolic dreams may seem whimsical, jumping from scene to scene, object to object, or situation to situation, if interpreted in their precise linear sequence, these dreams will lead us to the discovery of how, in fact, their linearity actually makes sense after they are interpreted. When I first discovered this, it kind of freaked me out how something seemingly so random was so acutely linear.

I'll never forget the time when, one night, before I went to bed, I asked my angels, "What's a good way for me to express my beliefs to others in a way that won't cut off their ears? After all, we all have different awareness and belief systems that we've learned throughout our lives and our individual beliefs, no matter what they are, our truth and also the truth of the universe, because of our connection to the Oneness. And in order for me to honor other people's beliefs and not be forceful, I need help in understanding a way to express myself that is beneficial in honoring not only my beliefs, but also the beliefs of others." Then I said to my angels, "I give you permission on all levels of my consciousness to help me with no limitations, to do whatever it takes to give me your opinion, in these matters in which I've asked for. So be it!"

That night, after I asked for help, my angels gave me a dream where I was walking down an old cobblestone road with the constant flow of people walking past me in the opposite direction. As I was walking, my consciousness outside of my body, was the observer, watching my every move, while still connected to the feelings and aware of the experiences and surroundings simultaneously.

I began to see myself spit several small natural pearls out of my mouth at the feet of the individuals as they were coming up toward me. I began taking note of how people reacted to the pearls I spat at their feet. Some people would just look at the pearl and then lift their head up and keep walking past it. Others would nudge it with their foot, stare at it for a little while and then proceed to walk by it. Still, others would pick it up, look at it and then throw it back down on the ground. One man stopped, picked up the pearl, looked at it and stuck it in his pocket. I followed this man to his house. My body went inside with him and my consciousness stayed outside and peered through a window as it watched me go into an empty room with old wooden floors and one chair in it. I grabbed the chair and pulled it to the center of the room, sat and waited for the old man to enter the room. When the old man entered the room, he brought a chair with him and sat at a distance facing me.

As I started speaking, the old man scooted his chair closer toward me and stared intensely into my face. I began shaking my head from side to side, like a model would in a long, shiny, healthy hair commercial. My hair rapidly grew out of my head and plummeted all the way down to the floor as thousands of natural pearls began falling out. Pearls covered the entire floor of the room and surrounded our feet, all the way up to our ankles.

This dream revealed to me that as I try to share my insights with others, it is best to spit a small pearl of love at their feet first and see what their reaction is to it. If their first reaction to it reflects that it isn't something they view as valuable or is something they can't see, then I talk about something else, like the weather or flowers. After all, our time is valuable and so is the time of the individuals we speak to. This dream helped me to honor and understand that. If for some reason the individual you're speaking to decides to pick up your pearl and stick it in their pocket, then let your hair out, as a symbolic gesture of giving them your pearls of wisdom.

Share your truth. Do this not for the reason of being better than others, being right or wrong, but for the reason of sharing a different perception of love in the possibility that the individual will take it and give themselves a leg up out of the darkness and into the light. We cannot alter or change a person's perception unless he or she wants us to. Our perceptions are our law and also the law of the universe. Perceptions we share with others may be interpreted differently based on their beliefs. We have absolutely no control or power over what they do with it.

Embracing and accepting what others do with the pearls as being that individual's responsibility will lead you toward understanding the concept of loving and giving allowance for all things in their own space and time, starting with yourself. The only responsibility we have involves first loving ourselves, utilizing what we are taught from Self-love, to set ourselves free and make a choice to present our pearls to others when the time presents itself and doing so, in a loving way for the respect and honor of other people's beliefs. The other thing this dream revealed to me is the role of the observer. I believe the observer is the

God within you that's learning and expanding throughout our lives through its experiences and journeys. That's why it is important for each one of us to be here and to live our unique combined journeys, as this expands the consciousness of what we would call, God.

I see our combined expansion of consciousness like this: Say somebody has an issue they're going through and through their unique perceptions, they discover a way to overcome it. It is at this moment their perception becomes like a newly created star in the universe, a new reality that embeds itself into the web of consciousness, which ultimately expands it and makes it bigger so that others can tap in to it and utilize it to help themselves. This belief coincides with the perception that there is no "there" to get to where you're going next. We are constantly expanding through our work and being helped through the work of others through our interconnectedness—as one.

Soul-traveling dreams

I believe that a soul-traveling dream is when your soul actually leaves the body and often are extremely vivid. This is possible because our soul isn't really earthbound. These types of dreams are normally intended to reveal the complexity of our soul and their interactions with the universe. We are not earthbound; our soul is constantly learning on multiple levels of consciousness and coexisting in other dimensions. By traveling to these other places, one can begin to see how curious our soul is in the quest to experience new realities and expansion.

As the curious soul we are, we oftentimes ask our angels on some level of our consciousness (either through the mind, soul, or spirit) to help us in learning new realities or in remembering old ones. We do this in order to help us find old hidden patterns that are working in the background and holding us back and to reveal to us and lead us to the greater truths and to the ever-increasing expansion of love.

The soul's constant curiosity can oftentimes lead us toward going to new worlds, meeting other beings, angels, coexisting energetic fields, other dimensions and meeting extra-terrestrials. This is all for the purpose of learning and our internal expansion of our consciousness. Most of the time we aren't aware we're even doing these things, but everybody does this kind of traveling whether we are aware of it or not. There is nothing to be afraid of because its natural. On the contrary, with these types of dreams, we can come back anytime we want, as we all do. After all, we all wake up in the morning in our bodies, ready to do what we need to do the next day. I find that our soul is very intelligent. This is evident when we consider we all come from the Oneness. In fact, often, we don't want to come back because we are having so much fun during our traveling. Don't worry, our Higher Self or even us thinking about our body, will bring us right back. By embracing the possibility in these perceptions, will allow us to increase our interactions with the Oneness.

Our interactions will grow and as they grow, we will begin to see them as truth. We will then believe in them, because they have become that which we have created in our own unique way. I know this may be a little hard to understand and sounds like a seemingly hard goal to achieve, but if we chose to contemplate soul-traveling to the point that we become aware of it, that would give it life inside of us and cause it to grow. Eventually, this leads us to no longer hold anything at arm's length and becoming more aware of our omnipresence. Becoming more aware of omnipresence, will lead to a shift in consciousness that will allow us to use focus and thought to no longer find it necessary to use cars, planes, buses, or any other form of transportation as we know it today, here on Earth. We will begin to use and be aware of our God-given gift, omnipresence and be able to travel anywhere in the universe and on our planet with just a thought.

Here's an example of a soul-traveling dream I had many years ago: In my dream, I was flying through a deep canyon and I noticed there was a cave on the left side close to the top of the canyon wall. I decided I wanted to fly into the cave to see what was in there. When I went into the cave, it was about sixty feet long and twenty feet wide and the complete bottom of the cave was full of a crystal clear, neon blue water and the water was lit up so that you could see the cave walls in its entirety. I dove down into the water as its depth was vast and as I came up, I noticed that there was two layers of water; one layer having a different temperature then the other and looked just like when freshwater meats salt water. When I reached the surface, I noticed a small ledge running the total length on one side of the cave walls and there was a young woman, maybe in her twenties, sitting on the ledge, just listing to her music through her headphones. I thought to myself, "Wow, this is cool place just to hang out for a little while." I just sat beside her on the ledge and just enjoyed looking at the water and feeling the temperature of the cave, until I felt extremely relaxed. I decided to go back to my body. To this day, I periodically will go into that cave in my meditation and just sit on that ledge and relax, deep breathing and staring at the water.

Contact dreams

The third type of dream is the contact-dream. That's where somebody will appear in the dream and maybe even call your name and talk to you on a one-to-one basis. These types of dreams are often very short and don't happen very often. They come with a very powerful punch, in how they make you feel. They're usually intense and extremely focused and oftentimes, reveal a finite and personalized message for the dreamer. The dreamer may even wake up feeling clear and empowered after a visitation dream because of the healing often received from this type of dream.

This is an example of two of my contact-dreams. I was asleep and not even aware that I was trying to astral project, as I often do. I noticed I was hovering in a very dark place, where not a single fragment of light even existed. All of a sudden, an elliptical form of light appeared in front of me and then opened up. There was a luminating, male humanoid looking being in a pure white robe standing in front of me with this very loving smile on his face. I could feel the energy of compassion emanating from his presence as he said to me, "Aw, don't worry, you are just trying to astral project." This experience revealed to me beyond a shadow of a doubt, how much we are truly loved and watched over. After this contact-dream, it gave me more of an incentive to work on astral projecting and taught me not to be so hard on myself and instead, have more compassion on myself, because I am like a little baby trying to learn something new.

The second contact dream I had, was at night. I was beginning to walk through a carnival and saw a Native American man in front of me. As I walked about twelve feet past him, he shouted out to me, "Lance, come here!" When I reached him, standing about a foot away, he leaned into me and got really close to my face, looked intently into my eyes and said in a strong voice, "Lance, you can have anything you want and then he handed me a red poker chip. After this dream, needless to say, I knew beyond a shadow of a doubt, that I could have anything I wanted and it gave me the incentive to focus on my abilities to manifest and in doing so, it wasn't a gamble, because the message was symbolized by the red poker chip.

Visitation dreams

Visitation dreams are unique because they normally don't require an interpretation of symbols. In other words, they're straight and to the point. For example, in one such dream, I was in a place that I would call the place where all things are created; it was a place of total darkness. When suddenly, a man appeared in front of me, like a beacon of light, looking at me with his body turned away, so I couldn't see the pendant he was wearing around his neck. All he said to me, with a very loving tone in his voice, was, "Oh, you're just trying to astral project, that's okay." This revealed to me his compassion and loving acceptance for me.

Just being in the presence of this visitation, helped me to learn and become more aware of the power of compassion and acceptance in myself and others. As for the pendant he was wearing, I got the sense he knew I used to be a jeweler and he didn't want me to see what he had, so I wouldn't recreate it. I believe some symbols can have a very powerful impact on the planet, as they can resonate on extremely high frequencies. The planet may not have been ready for these types of energies yet and the exposure of these energies in the form of a pendant in this case, could have caused a ripple effect of many non-pleasurable outcomes because of the energy's ability to rapidly ferret out what is not closely related to the pure forms of love the pendants symbol would create.

What I would recommend for a person beginning to interpret dreams is to purchase a book for interpreting dreams. My favorite dream book is called, *20,000 Dreams,* by Mary Summer Rain. There are many dream symbol interpretation books out there. The main thing is that the book you choose resonates with you. From my experience, I would highly recommend programing your book since you are going to use it as a tool.

Programming your dream book

I feel learning how to interpret dreams can be very important from a communication standpoint and it is well worth taking the time. When learning how to interpret symbolic types of dreams, you can either get a dream book or create your own meanings of the symbols. When using a dream book, I like to just use one book and program it. I program the book by holding it between my hands and speaking these words out loud: "I am choosing to use this book as a tool to help me interpret my dreams. I create that every dream I have, coincides with the definitions in this book with no limitations. So be it."

By doing this, you are actually programming your book and turning it into a finite tool. This is equivalent to telling the universe to be in cahoots with you. Think of it like working together as a team where everyone is on the same page. It will be uncanny how easy it will be to interpret your dreams after this step is taken. You can also interpret your dreams and dreams for others by utilizing your unique interpretations of what a symbol means to you. As long as you believe in your interpretation of a symbol, so does the universe and it will resonate in accordance.

Your interpretation of the symbol may not mean the same to somebody else or coincide with symbols in the books of others, but as long as you believe in it, so it is. The universe will keep utilizing that symbol over and over again, knowing that that's what it means to you. You will be amazed at its accuracy. You may find your dream book will reveal an attribute or issue that is hindering your growth and it was carried forward in you from a past life, in the form of cellular memories.

CHAPTER 12

Past lives and their influences

Before we start, on the deeper meanings of past lives, I want to give an example through my personal experience, on how I discovered and came to the belief in the existence of past lives. When I was thirteen years-old, I had my first glimmer of one of my former past lives, just prior to this life. I believed they existed only because they made sense to me when I started contemplating why I had so many innate abilities, that didn't fit into this life and wondered why I just knew so many things. I wondered why performing certain tasks such as hunting, trapmaking, friction fire making and knapping arrowheads, was so easy and I knew exactly how to do them without any lessons. I also couldn't understand why I innately loved and understood the ways of Native Americans and why it all felt so natural to me. For years, I would spend several hours of the day out in the desert with my bow and arrow, hunting, tracking, making friction fires and traps. I was extremely attuned to animals to the point where I could run them down and second-guess where they were going. In fact, at that same age, I was out in the desert hunting rabbits. I came across one and instead of shooting it with my arrow, I decided to run it down and catch it with my hands.

As I was running after the rabbit, I heard a voice in my head that sounded like me talking to myself, but it felt much stronger, saying, "The rabbit is going to turn to the left." So, I just made a forty-five-degree angled dash to the left and all of a sudden, the rabbit stopped and made a sharp left, right toward me. I could see the surprised look in the rabbit's eyes and sensing its shock that I was standing in its way.

After doing the same thing about five times, I could tell the rabbit was freaking out and getting tired. I couldn't figure out how I knew where it was going at all times; I just did. Then, at an instant, I heard the voice say, "The rabbit is going to stop and run right to you and all you have to do is pick it up."

I stopped dead in my tracks and just stood there with my heels touching each other, making a V formation. All of a sudden, the rabbit stopped running about twenty yards in front of me and turned around. It ran toward me and into my feet. His little nose wedged into my heels, while panting rapidly.

All I did was just reach down and picked him up. I remember I thought he was so cute, so I gave him a little kiss and said, "Thank you," and placed him back on the ground. He just sat there for a little bit and then slowly moved away. I stood there for a little while and wondered what had just happened. It took me several years before I realized that I was using something called, intuition. I just thought that was a normal thing to do.

About a week after the rabbit incident, I began to have a strong urge to make my own bow and arrows. I decided that I didn't want to use the store-bought ones anymore because it was just too easy. I wanted to give the animals more of a fair chance. I decided to make my own from scratch.

A vision of the past

This vision started at the age of fourteen when I decided to make my own bow and arrows. The traditional Recurve bow and arrows, after years of practice, became too easy for me. I decided I needed a little bit of a challenge. As I asked myself, "Why is it that, when I apply pressure with this dear antler on this piece of obsidian, in this particular spot, that I know exactly what will happen on the other side?" Right after asking this question, I felt like a wave of water rushing over my entire body, a kind of a déjà vu moment; like everything around me didn't exist, only a magnified moment in time. A moment I now know to be as an awakened trance. I turned my gaze and looked down at my arm and said to myself, in surprise and amazement, "What happened to me? I'm not supposed to be white! I'm a Native American!"

I stood there for about three minutes in amazement, staring at my arm and wondering why it was white. Then, just as suddenly as the feeling came, I snapped out of it, with only the memory of its occurrence left behind. This experience baffled me for several years afterward.

Encountering my spirit guide

About five years later, when I was eighteen, I spent the summer in a little two-story cabin in Idyllwild, California. One night, as I awakened from sleeping downstairs, I heard the voice of my mother speaking to somebody upstairs. I got out of my bed, got dressed and started walking upstairs to see who it was.

Walking up the stairs, my attention focused in on the creaking sound beneath my feet as I stepped on the pine stair slats leading to the top and the smell of the cedar-scented air from last night's fire became stronger and stronger, revealing to me that I was getting closer to the top. The room above that had the fireplace in it. When I arrived at the top, I noticed a small-statured woman with shoulder-length blond hair sitting next to my mother on the couch. At the instant we made eye contact with each other, instead of introducing herself to me, the woman shouted out with a voice of authority, "Lance, you need to go to a dentist right away! It's very important—you have a very bad tooth!" Needless to say, that tooth became abscessed later and as a result I ended up having to get a root canal.

Then she said, "Oh by the way, you have a spirit guide who is extremely close to you. In fact, he is almost inside of you. He won't reveal his name to me because he is very famous and if he did, everybody would know who he is. He says when you get older, he will reveal himself to you." When she said this, like I would normally do with things I didn't understand, I just took it as a grain of salt and put it in the filing cabinet inside of my mind.

About the age of fifteen, I had a dream where I was walking down a sidewalk toward an old white picket fence with its gate closed. Walking toward the gate, I looked over to my right side and saw a vast windblown golden field of wheat. The field mesmerized me as I watched the ripple effects the wind created blowing across the top of the landscape. All of a sudden, several Native Americans magically appeared before my eyes in the wheat field. They were all lined up in rows, military-style. They all began to chant in unison. During the chant, the first thing they did was pat their hands on the center of the chest, known as the heart center, three times. Each hand went in unison down to the knees and patted three times on the kneecaps. Ending with three claps out in front of their chest. They just kept doing the same thing over and over again, in synchronized hand motions—all as one.

I began to follow them, mimicking their chants and movements. All the while, I was still walking forward down a straight concrete sidewalk leading to a white gate at its end. All of a sudden, I noticed a figure approaching the closed gate on the opposite side of me. It was a little blurry at first, slowly emerging into view. The closer we came together, the more he came into focus. I could see clearly now that he was an old Native American man. He proceeded to open the gate and started walking toward me.

As I walked toward him, I peered down on the ground about a foot to my right side and noticed a little baby lying there on the ground. At the same time, the Native American man came closer and said, "Is the little baby ready to graduate yet?" I said, "Yes." Right after I said yes, the Native American man and I sat down. He was at my back-left side. I glanced down to my left side, next to my hip and noticed some pinion nuts. I picked them up in my left hand and reached back to share some with him. When I gave him the pinion nuts, my fingertips brushed across the palm of his hand and it felt like leather.

It was at this moment that I noticed the chanting had stopped in the background. I quickly looked in front of me and I noticed that all the people had magically disappeared. I looked down at my feet and the baby also had disappeared. I turned around and looked behind me and the man was gone.

Suddenly, a tremendous amounts of emotions overcame me and I felt very sad. I leapt to my feet and literally dove down to the ground like you would if you were diving onto a baseball diamond. I scooped up the dirt in a hugging fashion bringing it to my heart from the spot where he had been sitting. As I was bringing the dirt vigorously and repeatedly to my heart, I started crying my eyes out. I shouted out loud in extreme sadness, "Grandpa, Grandpa, please don't leave me again! I love you, Grandpa!"

I woke up, still crying my eyes out, while experiencing profound feelings of sadness. I got out of bed and went to talk to my girlfriend, who was a professional psychic. Before I even mentioned anything about the dream, she said to me, "My angels told me to get you this book for your birthday." When she gave it to me, I looked at the front cover and noticed that it pictured the same Native American man who was in my dream!

Nurturing the seeds of past lives

The instant I noticed he was the same guy, the memory of what the other psychic had told me fifteen years prior at the cabin in Idyllwild, came flooding back to me like a great mighty river. I realized the book I received for my birthday was the biography of my grandfather from my past life prior to this one in the 1800s. She had said he would reveal himself to me when I got older. I thought, "Wow, now everything is starting to make perfect sense to me!" I could see now why I knew how to make arrowheads, fires, bows and arrows, traps, pottery and how talk to animals.

Suddenly, another thought came rushing into my mind: "Well, if this is the biography of my grandfather, then that would mean that there are probably some photos of his family members in it. That means, there might also be photo of me and my family members in this book!" I started looking through the book at all the pictures and came to several photos where I saw people who were in my family in this lifetime. I was amazed how little our looks change from lifetime to lifetime. Needless to say, seeing this totally blew me away!

I finally found the photograph I was most interested in finding. I saw my grandfather sitting next to a young woman with a little baby in her arms and to my amazement, a deep feeling of connectedness came over me and at that moment, I realized that the little baby in the arms of the woman who looked to be about twenty years old, was me! I drew my gaze to the mother of the little baby and suddenly became overwhelmed with an inner knowingness and a rush of energy coming up from my feet and out through the top of my head, as I then spoke out loud, "Oh my God, I know her! That's my daughter in this lifetime. "Wow—she even looked the same way she does in this life!" Then another loud thought came to my mind that said, "Go and take this book to your daughter and show her this photo to see what she thinks about it."

I took the book over to my daughter and without trying to influence her, I said to her, "Look at that woman sitting on the bench with the little baby in her arms. Doesn't she look familiar?" Suddenly, my daughter went into the same awakened trance-like state I did when I was thirteen years old and with a dazed look in her eyes, she said, "Wow, she looks a lot like me!"

I said, "She does, doesn't she—isn't that interesting?" I closed the book, not saying anything, allowing my daughter to come to her own conclusions about what she had just experienced. After closing the book, it was like a light switch flipped on inside of me as the seed of past lives had been deeply planted into my consciousness. I began to water my new seed with my thoughts and an array of questions of what reincarnation meant to me.

As the plant started to grow, it began to bump and push its way up through the doubts and disbeliefs of my mind's soil. It finally made its way up through the soil into my consciousness. It was at this time I felt a complete knowingness in the existence of past lives. This is what I call the born-again moment or, *a new leaf on the tree of consciousness.* We can be born again several times in a lifetime. Being born again simply means that a new reality has come into our consciousness that changes us and causes us to live and react in different ways than we did before.

I felt like that book was a time capsule just waiting until I was old enough to understand. It also showed me how much my grandfather loved me and how much we are all loved—that someone would leave a part of himself or herself here, so that we could learn about the existence of past lives and come to the realization that nobody ever dies. We live on forever and forever is a very long time!

As a footnote, the reality of past lives also revealed itself to me in my later years. Don't worry about getting it or understanding it all in this lifetime. We often put ourselves through a lot of turmoil and chaos by beating ourselves up because we feel are not getting it, understanding it, or going fast enough. The truth is, we live forever and the wisdom and knowledge of an awareness will always be there and start at the beginning. There is an infinite expansion, expression and multiple facets in every truth. So, you see, a new reality will always be the tip of the iceberg, which ultimately means that there is no "there" to get to, wherever are you going to get, next.

The secrets of the past are revealed

After I became aware of the existence of past lives, I frequently started having dreams revealing many of my lives in the past. Realizing the existences of past lives has led me to understand the profound influences those lives have had not only on myself, but also on every one of us. As the secrets of my past were revealed, many things in my current life started to make total sense. I felt like a big burden had been lifted off my shoulders. I could see with total clarity why I felt, acted and lived the way I did and why I chose the parents, friends, jobs, circumstances, wives and realities in my life.

Another thing that was revealed to me was why at the beginning of my youthful years, I never hung around with white people. I had always wondered why all of my friends were different ethnicities. Then it came to me: "No wonder why I came back as a white man in this lifetime. In my Native American lifetime, the white man did terrible things to my family, which caused the integration of a belief that all white men had bad hearts. I was born again this lifetime in the race I had negative beliefs toward, so I could learn that it doesn't matter what race a person is. What matters is how much we can receive and give love."

My extensive inner quest in discovering my past lives and the influences they have had on me has led me to many great discoveries. One of the greatest discoveries I've had is the realization that we live in the past and in order to be free, we must work hard to release the past. Only by living in the now, can we finally be free.

The power of setting past lives free

As I mention before, we are greatly influenced by our past lives. Due to of our past lives, we choose our parents, our race, our health, where we are born, who our friends are, our life experiences and our circumstances. Things like phobias, prodigies, birthmarks, physical, mental, emotional, deformities, beliefs and DNA structures all come from past-life experiences. That being said, I thought I would share this example of how a past life can create certain circumstances that on the surface oftentimes are viewed as negative experiences. Let's say that in a past life there was a pregnant Native American woman who was sitting on a rock next to a river getting a drink of water. Suddenly somebody rushes up to her, kills her and cuts the baby out of her stomach. Back in those days, that was not an uncommon practice. From that moment forward, a fear-based memory is etched into the consciousness of the mother and her unborn child.

These types of occurrences for many souls are exactly what creates certain fears toward such things as moving forward, seeking self-awareness, being yourself and even being born. Not only do these life-altering circumstances have lasting effects on our soul's life here on Earth, but they also influence the way our soul interacts when we leave our bodies and go to the other side.

These types of soul-altering circumstances oftentimes are what keep us in the circle of reincarnation. Until we can break away from the bondage of our past and feel worthy of love, peace, joy, happiness and balance, we will just keep coming back. Think about this: in the universe, there are more souls than there are stars in the heavens and they have all gone through certain traumas and experiences in their past lives.

In the case of this little Native American baby's past-life experience, what if all that soul had to do in this lifetime in order to set itself free from the fear and blockages of its past life (coming from when it was cut out of its mother's womb) was to go past the point of the birth process right before the baby was cut out of the mother's womb in its past life? What if all it had to do was get past the fear of the rebirthing process of that point in order to set itself free so that soul could increase its abilities to receive increased perceptions of love? This type of challenge oftentimes can account for stillborn children.

Even the mother is frequently the same mother as in the past life. Out of extreme love for the soul of her baby, the mother chose before she came here, to have the same soul return to her womb, in order to help the soul to move past a certain phase of the birth process. This will help break the trauma cycle. Due to the baby progressing past a certain term, the soul in that baby was set free from the past trauma and the mother was also set free, because it allowed the mother to experience the loss of her child in a different way. This causes a shifting of the previous extreme experience, to one even though painful, to a new more acceptable outcome that doesn't have as much of an emotional punch as the other one. This will also change the DNA lineage for the mother and the child at the same time. In fact, after a miscarriage, the soul of the baby can now go onto experience other forms of learning or it can come back again in the same mother and be perfectly healthy and fine. The soul will no longer have the fear to go past a certain phase of the pregnancy and the mother will no longer feel the fear, guilt and hopelessness of being pregnant and losing her child. This is a small glimpse into how we help one another be set free from past experiences in our cellular memories and how much we love one another.

In seeking the possibility of past lives, one will dissolve the illusion of judgment and begin to grow even more aware of the truth in the Oneness. Letting go of judgment will free us from its bondage.

CHAPTER 13

The bondage of judgment

The bondage of judgment, for self and others, has entered into our consciousness from generation to generation and from lifetime to lifetime, to the point that we are even born with it embedded into our DNA. Like I said before in an earlier chapter, we are similar to a breed of dog, all of us with our inherent characteristics. Nobody has to tell us to judge others or ourselves. We just do it without being aware of the ripple effects it creates within ourselves and others. By eliminating judgment in our lives, we will begin to live in the freedom of love, peace, joy, abundance and balance, way beyond our wildest dreams and imaginations.

Judgment makes us stuck

By choosing to allow judgment as part of our inherent patterns, we literally enslave ourselves into seemingly unbreakable circular patterns represented as what we believe to be as real in such forms as reincarnation, karma, guilt, shame, fear, low self-esteem and wars. "Karma" simply involves an individual who hasn't chosen to let go of the past in ways such as judgment, forgiveness of self and forgiveness of others. We don't forgive ourselves, so we beat ourselves up internally for the things that we did or somebody else did to us in the past. Due to this cancerous internal conflict, the universe just re-creates it. The universe is both the dark and the light. We aren't separate from the universe. The universe only does what we focus on. In fact, the universe only sees these old thought patterns from the past as a command and nothing else. They are not good or bad, right or wrong—just a command. By constantly conjuring old realities from the past, we will literally recreate a repetitive motion. We will keep re-creating old situations and bring them into the present over and over again. This occurs not only in this lifetime, but we can also carry it over to our future lifetimes. The question here is, how can we let go of the past, so we don't keep recreating scenarios over and over again that bring us pain and sorrow? What I did was change my perception about when something negative happened to me. I did this by not getting on my old hamster wheel. I chose to view the situation as a mirror.

By transmuting judgment into the form of the mirror and viewing it as a reflection of self and by taking into consideration the possibility of the Oneness (meaning the person we are judging is not separate from us), one will get an honest outward reflection of our inner realities. This could mean both the desirable and non-desirable inner realities.

Learning to transmute judgment

One technique I like to use to help transmute judgment into love and acceptance and find the secret hidden truth to my inner reality, is to view what I see in the other person's situation that I'm judging, as one of my socks. In other words, they and I, are wearing the same socks, just a different color. By being honest and associating the judgment, I see in the other, as my own sock. It points my consciousness in a desired and focused direction best suitable leading to my inner truth.

Another technique I like to use is, after I catch myself judging somebody else, is to go home and sit in my favorite meditation chair take a few deep breaths to relax and clear my mind. I begin comparing my sock with the sock the other person is wearing. After a few minutes of breathing and comparing my reality to their observed reflection of me, feelings or situations from the past will start to emerge. Eventually, using this process, I finally discovered we were both wearing the same sock, the only difference between my sock is that it was blue and the other person were red. If we are honest about ourselves and look deeply within, we will find the match. This will lead us to understand the mirror truly exists and the reflected blessing of self-discovery, or the truth. And the truth will set you free.

I have discovered through my personal evolutionary process that all things that I once judged in other people, without an exception and no matter how severe it seemed to be, has always been revealed to be a direct reflection of my inner reality. It was either in the same form, or a uniquely different one. For me, when I choose not to view judgment as judgment anymore and choose to see it in the form of the mirror, I began to realize why I was implementing my inherent form of judgment as part of my daily process in the first place. It revealed to me that judgment is fairy dust, meaning, it doesn't exist. The only thing that truly exist is the mirror.

I discovered I was using judgment as a way to sweep my feelings about myself under the carpet in order to use it like a drug of choice to make me feel better about myself. I did this because my feelings were too hard to deal with. It reminded me of when I was a kid and felt uncomfortable playing in the sandbox with the other kids because of what they were doing and what they thought of me. I tried to use judgment in order to make them feel more uncomfortable than I did, so that I could feel powerful. However, all the while, I was not getting rid of the things that were making me uncomfortable in the first place.

When I realized integrating the reality of the mirror and what I was seeing, is simply reflecting to me my unseen, deep issues. Life all of a sudden got extremely easy for me because I knew beyond a shadow of a doubt, that I could always depend on the mirror to lead me to the truth and that if something bothered me about somebody else, it told me more about me than it did about them. Which ultimately leads to the discovery of how much we are truly loved, connected and do for each other and how important it is for each one of us to be here on this school called planet Earth. In order to be our own unique selves, even though sometimes people don't agree with what they see, our reflections are priceless.

I now see things in a different way and can truly say, "Wow! The person I judged in the past must really love me and I am so grateful for their reflection of me, because of the gift they have given me through their reflection. I can now seize the opportunity to heal the unseen things that have been ailing me my whole life. Thank you so much—I love you."

By eliminating judgment, it also dissolved all of its tentacles and their connections that were playing in the background of my consciousness, such as shame, fear and low self-esteem. This enhanced my ability to channel love in a purer form and become love, which enabled me to assist myself and the planet without going through all the filters of judgment.

Choosing to let go of judgment

We all channel divine love in its purest form. The reason why it comes out a little clunky at times (such as in the forms of rape, murder, judgment, war, addictions, pain and suffering) is because of the path our pure divine channel of love has to pass through before it expresses itself. By eliminating the filtering elements of the past through the self-realization of our inner existence, we can make a choice to let them go and in doing so, become increasingly able to channel love in the purest form possible.

By choosing a path of letting go of judgment, as well as aggressions toward us and aggression from others from the past, not only will we drastically change our experiences in this life, but we will also drastically change our future life experiences if we chose to come back in physical form because of its altering influence on our DNA. It will also allow us to experience different life lessons if we chose to come back to this school and again, choose our parents, childhood experiences and life circumstances. The biggest thing we tend to judge is ourselves. Constantly beating ourselves up by saying things to ourselves such as, "I'm stupid and not good enough," and even the unseen inner awareness of our past lives tends to play havoc inside of our consciousness. Below is a technique I used to help let go of self-judgment and help me to have a better understanding of the past. It gave me the ability to let go of my past because by using this technique, it gave me the insight to see how the angelic realm truly saw things instead of the worldly perspective.

Exercise: Technique to release judgment

One of the greatest ways I discovered to let go of judgment of myself and of others was through the understanding of my past-life experiences. The reason why past lives can harness facets of judgment of others and self, is because of the traumatic events that can still be running amuck in our subconscious. Past lives can be so allusive, they can oftentimes be difficult to find by yourself without assistance from a past life regressionist. At times I'm able to get a twinge of their existence when I feel disturbances in my force that don't pertain to anything that happened in this lifetime and I can't find any reference point. At this point, I will normally sit in a chair and take several deep breaths to get in touch with my feelings to bring them to focus so that I can discover what it is that's bothering me. I start by pulling the feeling toward me and being consumed by it, until it reveals itself to me. After I did this technique, for example in one case, I found out that I felt hopeless.

Once I found the gold nugget that I was feeling hopeless, I knew what it was I needed to release. Before I went to bed, I would say out loud, "I give my angels permission on all levels of my consciousness with no limitations to reveal to me through repetitive dreams why I feel so hopeless at times and I give you permission to keep giving me the same dream over and over again, until I completely understand my question." This technique of asking questions has always had a profound impact on increasing my understanding and self-awareness. It can actually be used in all matters of life such as, health, foods to eat, what should I do next, finding your life's purpose and many more.

Through accessing dreams and utilizing this technique, I learned that even the saintly of saints and holiest of holies have murdered, raped, tortured and have done all kinds of unthinkable things to the many, rather than the few, in this life and their past lives.

When I came to the awareness that we all have done what our society would call "the unthinkable," I asked my angels why I had done all of those bad things, because inside it makes me feel like I am always doing something wrong and causes me to hesitate in life. The answer they gave, with a cry in their voice, was, "How could you think you have ever done anything wrong?" After they gave me that answer, of course, I felt so relieved, like a big weight had been lifted off my shoulders.

This process revealed to me that the same is true for everybody from the beginning of their entire existence. After I realized this, I replied to my angels by saying, "Oh, great. That's going to really go over well. How am I going to explain that to the world?" So that night, I had a dream that gave me the understanding of why it's important for each one of us to go through our individual processes, regardless of how it may look and be perceived by others.

In the dream, I was in a pitch-black tunnel. I couldn't see a thing. I reached up high above my head with my arms fully extended upward while touching the walls. I couldn't help but feel how slimy it was. I began to walk forward, suddenly, a monster that looked like a Tyrannosaurus Rex appeared in front of me. It had its back toward me and it started walking deeper into the tunnel, coaxing me to follow it by periodically looking back at me.
As I followed it, my hands were sliding across the slimy walls of the tunnel. I could feel the walls becoming smaller and smaller. I noticed that the Tyrannosaurus was also getting smaller and smaller.

Without warning, at the end of the tunnel, a small little door appeared made of defined white light. It was like something you might see in, *Alice in Wonderland*. The door opened as an illuminating, great white light came raging through the dark tunnel, like a great mighty river. I then proceeded to walk through the door. As I entered the room full of white light, an angel was standing next to me on my right-hand side.

I spoke to the angel and said, "Don't tell me that was a man inside of a monster suit." Then, lo and behold, here came this little Tyrannosaurus approximately three feet tall. He walked up to me and pulled off his head, revealing a small man inside and in doing so, he replied by saying, "Of course I'm a man in a monster's suit. How else do you think I could've gotten through that big black tunnel?"

After having this dream, I completely forgave everybody of their aggressions against me and the self-blame, shame and inflicted pain, I had projected upon myself for what I had done to others in the past. I also learned the reason why nobody has ever done anything wrong. It is because even though we may view what a person does as being something wrong and for good reason, the truth is, for that particular soul, it was required for its unique journey and timing of awareness. In order for it to evolve and come into the light, it first needed to go into the darkness in order to come into the light, to set itself free, like some of us are today. That's why we know that murdering, war, fighting and destroying the planet, isn't a desirable outcome for ourselves and for others. We did those things because we had already done that dark stuff in the past and we are done with it. Other souls still need to finish these darker paths in order to evolve, find inner love, peace and the Oneness.

We have to go through the dark to get to the Light

This Tyrannosaurus dream helped me realize that in order to find the light at the end of the tunnel, which is love beyond our wildest dreams and imaginations, we have to be the monster and go through the big dark tunnel first. We must also shift our perception of the darkness, from being a place that's evil, to giving it a big hug and a kiss and accept it as an ally as part as our process leading to the light. After all, if we didn't feel the pain of the darkness, then what would give us the incentive to seek or go into the light? From this dream, I learned that there is nobody, not one single person on this entire planet, who has truly ever done anything wrong and that being said, it also means that there's not a single soul on this planet, not even Gandhi or Mother Teresa, who doesn't have mud on their feet. Otherwise, what would be the purpose of going to the hardest school in the universe we call, planet Earth?

This doesn't mean we can just do anything we want to other people, life forms, or the planet and not care. It simply means we are trying to find an inner pristine form of love, known as, *Heaven on Earth*. We are babies and don't understand yet how to find this love. We do things without even knowing why. Our life experiences and actions will eventually be revealed in their unique individual forms and in due time, this inner pristine love we are all looking for, will reveal itself to us. In other words, we will all in time, eventually find the true feeling of heaven within and be the love were looking for and desire to see in others.

Through calamity we can find the Oneness

Here's an example of a situation that happened here on Earth that created a drastic change in the consciousness of humanity. That day was 9-11. In my opinion, even though this day was a seemingly horrific occurrence, it was one of the greatest catalysts of love that the world has ever seen. The reason why I view it this way, is because of my beliefs that you are the creator, never the victim. If we decided to look at this scenario through the eyes of nonjudgment and the belief that we are never the victim, but always the creator, how would that feel? Coming from this viewpoint, I believe before the so-called victims and their perpetrators were born on planet Earth, they had one mission in life and that was to bring in a much higher level of love.

What if they got together in the place, we call the heavenly realm and said to one another, "Wow, we are still having wars and killing people and doing bad things to each other. We really need to do something that will bring in more of an awareness of love to this planet, so that we all can move forward and get past all of this hate, prejudice, judgment and war. What do we need to do?" Then one said, "What do you think of this as a solution? How about if we get some of our buddies together and let's see what we can do together as a team, something that would create the greatest ripple effect of love for everyone on Earth and the universe?"

So, they had a great counsel; the so-called victims and the so-called perpetrators were in cahoots together. They devised a plan to bring to the earth, the awareness of other levels of love. One said, "I'll fly the plane into the building." The other said, "I'll be the passenger." "Yes," said another, "I feel that is a good plan. What do you guys think?" And they all agreed, "Okay, let's do it!"

They were all born here on Earth for the sole purpose to do what had to be done, because the timing was right to usher in these higher levels of divine love. For me, it took some time to ingest the possibility that this seemingly bad thing was done for us out of profound love. Due to my belief that nothing happens to us, it only happens *for* us, made it easier for me to see it as a high possibility and then, combined with knowing that nobody really dies and that we are all immortal, meaning we all live forever. After contemplating these things for a while, I began to see the mastery in the timing of the whole thing and the urgency for the need to change the awareness of humanity.

After a while, it was obvious to me, when I saw the impact it had on the mass consciousness, in regard to the heart openings generated from the wave of love they unselfishly gave us on that day. What did all eyes see and hearts feel as the black man held the white man in his arms and vice versa? We saw how much profound love we have for each other; how precious life is and how much we needed to change so something like this could never happen again. Also, we saw that all races were helping one another and there was no existence of prejudice, gender differences or judgment. At that moment, it all went out the door and revealed the truth. The only thing that exists is love!

In the Bible, it says, "My ways aren't your ways. Many are my ways. Having a heart of rigidness and not that of clay, will make it difficult to find the foundation of love and will hinder the earthly existence of heaven."

What if, in the case of 9-11, after it was all said and done, the so-called perpetrators and victims were on the other side, bawling their eyes out in feelings of extreme love, having a big party and shouting out loud, "We did it! Love has been accelerated and there's no going back now!" Sometimes the only way we can find love and have the ability to see its existence, is through the glasses of pain and suffering. I will say this: if one chooses to take into consideration these words I have shared as a possibility, the sheer acceptance will lead to rapid acceleration in discovering the existence of love as it is revealed to us, in this form. Even in times of war, we can always find the love within ourselves and others; ultimately discovering the Oneness in All.

CHAPTER 14

The effects of war

How does what we do affect the planet and its inhabitants? The answer to this question becomes evident when one takes into consideration that planet Earth is alive and has a consciousness. Due to our interconnectedness, meaning the oneness of all life, everything that occurs on planet Earth, occurs within each one of us.

Yes—this means that when we do destructive things to the planet, such as detonate bombs, kill people and poison the Earth, the ripple effect it has on the planet and the mass consciousness is profound. Everything we do to one another and our planet, we are literally doing to ourselves. When we negatively impact our planet, Mother Earth, in turn feels sad, disrupted, cancerous, unsettled and off-balance. This translates into us feeling the same way. Remember—that which we have done to others we have done unto ourselves. I believe that this is the reason why we are going through great waves of sadness, cancer, uneasy feelings and imbalance. The Earth is not separate from us. If we heal the Earth, we too, in turn will be healed. On the same note, if each one of us take the responsibility to heal ourselves, our combined efforts will literally heal the planet.

Planet Earth is alive

I referred to this before: In the Bible, there is a story about Jesus. When he was asked by the soldiers to tell the people to stop clapping and shouting his name out in a joyful manner, Jesus replied by saying, "If I told them to stop, the very rocks would start doing the same." He also said, "If you told the tree to get up and plant itself into the ocean, it would listen to you and do it."

My point is, if it were true that these seemingly inanimate objects had no consciousness, then how is it that they could listen to what Jesus said and respond? Maybe the lessons behind his words were given to us simply to help dissolve the illusion of separateness. They are revealing to us that all things have a consciousness, while at the same time, asking us to increase communication with all living things. All is alive, has a consciousness and is working together as one. Here's food for thought: Many years ago, I was sitting under a tree when I had a realization and said, "The trees are the lungs of mother earth, the rivers are her blood veins, the clouds are her kidneys, the ocean is her heart and the bugs, plants and animals are her immune system." I began to think, "Well, what would happen if we didn't let go of our greed and didn't stop polluting Mother Earth?" The answer that came to me was: She has a way of reclaiming herself and one way she may do it, is that when she purges herself through the other aspects of herself, meaning her immune system such as, humans, plants, bugs and water. Even now, as you are reading these words, the mosquitoes are laying their eggs in poisoned water and getting mosquito viruses and then biting us and the animals. We eat animals that are getting poisoned by the chemicals that is in their food, coming from the environment. All I'm saying is, don't be surprised if something as small as an insect can create havoc, however, when we embrace stewardship of our dear planet, we can literally co-create heaven on Earth. Even when we leave this Earthly existence, we never die, we live forever and ever.

CHAPTER 15

When we die

The main reason for this chapter is to share a perception that, if one chooses to embrace it, has the ability to lessen the impact of losing a precious loved one. I can't tell you how many times people have come to me after the loss of their loved ones, maybe five, ten, fifteen years later, still living in sadness, as if their loved one had just passed away; yesterday. The loss of a loved one can cause the ones left behind to hold back from life, to be afraid to embrace love again and to share their love with the many, rather than the few. I will say this with all certainty: absolutely *nobody* ever dies!

Death means a new experience

We live for eternity and eternity is a very long time. Choosing not to let go of our loved ones when they pass literally hinders our ability to move forward into the greater possibilities of love, truth and awareness.

Oftentimes, the message I get from the other side when people come to me after losing a loved one, is how sad the deceased loved one is to see that the ones they left, are unhappy and holding themselves back from embracing love and life again. In contrast, where the deceased ones are, they're having fun, living their existence with their other loved ones, in the heavenly frequency, or *the other side,* as some may call it.

Life is good and those on the other side realize that they still can interact and have communication with us on this side; it's just in a different form. We will always have opportunities to be with our loved ones in forms such as reincarnation, visitations through our dreams and visitations in other forms such as, animals, plants, the insect realm and many more. For example: Many people have reported a respective recurrence of certain animals, birds, rocks in the shape of a heart, objects or incidences that keep recurring quite frequently, through their life, that will remind them of the loved one they feel they lost. When this happens, most people just shake it off as a coincidence. I assure you; it is not. Remember, in order to experience new realities, we must first change our perceptions into new unused perceptions/realities before we can experience a more full and abundant life. Another thing that helped me was when I realized that the place where we go when we cross over, is what we would call, heaven. Here on Earth, it is a frequency/vibration and that heaven isn't a place way up in the sky, in the clouds; it's here, coexisting on Earth. It is just on a different vibration, where all are here and we will forever be together. Remember, we are here to dissolve the illusion of separateness. That means we are already on the other side. That's why it's so easy for our loved ones who have crossed over, to communicate to us, through these forms from the other side. Another thing that's hard to grasp for most of us is death itself. It has been my experience that we all die every night when we go to sleep and every time we wake up in the morning, we are literally making a choice to do so, mainly because we have more work or learning to do here. We leave our bodies every time we go to sleep or take a nap. This could be considered a form of "death."

I like to think of dying as like opening a door to a different room and when you open it, you have a whole new experience—not a lesser one than the one you had here on Earth. It's just a continuation of the same. We come here to Earth to dissolve the illusion of separateness, to increase communication with all living things and to receive and give love. This ultimately leads to a heightened sense of awareness that will increase our abundant prosperity, when we move to the next level—in this case, the place we go when we die.

We create our own death

There are two phrases that have helped me tremendously in dealing in the loss of loved ones: "It is through our choices and perceptions that we create our reality" and "Never were you the victim, but always the creator." This means to me, that on some level, the person who died had a say in the matter, regardless of what happened. You may never know what our loved ones did in their past lives and what gifts they're giving to the ones they leave behind. It's all about the lessons and nothing happens to us, it happens *for* us. This means that by seemingly dying and experiencing the emotions and the unique thought processes of what an individual may contemplate after their loved one passed, could be assisting the loved ones left behind to see value in other aspects of their lives, such as a heightened sense of love, connections with family members, letting go of the past and so on. All for the sole purpose of assisting and leading to the true heavenly experience, meaning, inner love, inner peace, inner balance and abundance way beyond our wildest dreams and imaginations. You know, Heaven on Earth!

I want to take this moment to share with you an experience in my life that was very revealing for me about death and its connection to our choices. When I was about thirty-four years old, I was heading southbound on Interstate 179 in Sedona, Arizona, suddenly, I noticed a defined ball of white light about the size of a golf ball moving at a quick pace, at approximately a forty-five-degree angle, in front of the grill of a semi-truck, that was coming in the opposite direction I was traveling. As this ball of light caught my attention, I noticed that right behind it (approximately three feet) was a sparrow flying at exactly the same path and speed that the ball of white light was traveling. As I watched the truck smash into the sparrow and the puff of its feathers flying everywhere, I made the connection and realized that the ball of light was the spirit of the sparrow.

This revealed to me a very interesting insight—the sparrow already knew it was going to get smashed and be blown into a thousand little pieces, even before it got hit. It made a choice and left its body. So, you see, the sparrow didn't feel a thing. It was already gone, which caused me to wonder whether we could do the same thing; if we could leave our bodies at will. In fact, I believe we can and often do, especially when we're asleep. Once, the angels told me in a dream that we are not earthbound. This makes sense to me, especially when you consider omnipresence.

We leave our bodies when we sleep

Here's another true story that happened to me at a very dark moment in my life. One day while living in Scdona, I was feeling extremely depressed. It was after a divorce and everything just seemed to be happening all at once. I said to myself, "I don't have to be here if I don't want to. I can leave here anytime I want; all I have to do is just leave me staying here. It is my choice anyway." I then said, "Besides that, I could just get my keys and throw them out the door. Nobody would ever know or care that I'm gone anyway."

I went into my bedroom and laid down on the bed with my hands underneath my pillow and in less than five minutes I went to sleep. At the same time as I was going through the process of going to sleep, I was consciously trying to move out of my body until I did it. When I was out of my body, I turned around and saw my body lying on the bed. I said to myself, "Yahoo, I did it! I told you I could do it!" and then started walking down the hallway.

All of a sudden, these two invisible hands hit my shoulders with extreme force and my soul flew back falling to the floor, on my knees and landed at the foot of the bed. As I knelt there, looking at my body lying on the bed, I decided I wanted to go back into my body because I felt like I had something I needed to do before I left. Needless to say, that was an interesting sensation.

The point of this story is: I did it. This tells me that we have the ability to leave our bodies at will as we do when we sleep. One thing this experience taught me, is that if someday when I get older and for some reason, I am lying in bed with all those tubes sticking in my arm, I decided that I'm not going to fight death and just make a decision to leave out of love for myself and for the love of others.

One more point to add is, people who are depressed sleep a lot. This is not saying people who sleep a lot are depressed. Sleeping is a form of escape and a form of healing for people with depression. During sleep, the depressed person leaves their body and goes to school on the other side or meets with their guides to learn about options to better themselves or change their perspective to process themselves to a happier state of being.

My meditation

I'll never forget the first time I ever meditated. The reason why I am mentioning this experience is because it usually takes a person several attempts to achieve what I did on the first time. I just sat down on the floor, at the base of my couch, with my back against the front of the couch and my legs in the lotus position, or Indian style, as some would call it, not following any studied technique and closed my eyes. I started breathing deeply and became extremely aware of my body. I focused on how much I could make my body relax. After deep breathing and constantly telling the stiff parts of my body to relax, I began to focus my inner gaze at my third eye and then suddenly, I started to notice these random colors, as if I were looking out through my third eye.

Intuitively, I decided to embrace the colors and become them as I started imagining myself flying into them, like *Superman*. I began to realize I could change the colors into anything I wanted. I changed the colors to yellow, to green and to purple. Each time I changed the colors, I would fly into them using my imagination. After a while of flying into the colors, I began to notice a buzzing sound and sensation throughout my body. I decided to embrace the sound and let it consume me and I noticed that by doing so, the sound and vibration feeling got stronger and stronger. I began to hear a whooshing noise as I saw myself flying through a thick fog. At that moment, I heard and felt an even stronger whooshing sound and to my amazement, I realized I was out of my body and flying over a pristine lagoon.

The water didn't have a ripple on it. I felt extremely peaceful as I flew about a foot above the top of the water's surface toward an island. My gaze became focused upon a single, huge, ancient tree with a deeply gnarled trunk. As I focused on the tree, the tree became my accelerant, rapidly drawing me closer to its base.

I now realized as I was getting closer to the tree, an old lady was sitting at its base. She was hard to see at first because her skin resembled the bark of the tree and her shoulder-length hair was as white as snow. As I was moving ever closer toward her, I spoke out loud and said, "Wow, do you see that?" and then, suddenly, I zapped right back into my body.

Boy, was I upset! It took a really long time for me to be able to get to that point in meditation and it made me feel like I robbed myself. I later realized that it taught me a good lesson of how to navigate future experiences. Now, when something bizarre happens when I meditate, I don't say anything, because I don't want to zap back real fast. I want to stick around for a while and ask questions. Regardless, the experience was very revealing in the plethora of knowledge it had to offer in relation to the symbols it presented.

One of the things I learned from this experience was that even though death can be sad, because of how much we love each other, death is not really that big of a thing. We really don't go anywhere and die. We leave are bodies thousands of times throughout our lives either unconsciously or consciously, through certain types of meditations. The only thing that matters and has influence over us, is our beliefs of what death means to us.

For me, one of the feelings I received after this out-of-body experience was that we're only here for a blink of an eye. We stay here as long as we can and as long as we choose to. All we need to do is to consider that we were never the victims, but always the creators. That means to me that no matter what, we are always going to be okay and nothing bad in the sense of the big picture, is ever going to happen to us. We are deeply and profoundly loved. We are the ones who create our realities and have the ability to expand way beyond our wildest dreams and imaginations! Even when a person ends their own life, love prevails and assists them into the Oneness.

CHAPTER 16

When a person commits suicide

Although this may be a tough subject to discuss, I think it is important, because I realize there are many individuals who have thought of doing this very thing. I will include an email conversation I had with a client regarding this subject. First, I would like to go over some different scenarios for souls that commit suicide, in order to present a contrast to the primary perception that everybody who commits suicide goes directly to hell.

First of all, as I mentioned in an earlier chapter, heaven and hell aren't a place we go when we die; they're a feeling. Everybody who commits suicide has the same opportunity to go into the Light as does everybody else. In other words, there is no hierarchy. That exists only in the illusion of separateness. The primary reason a soul doesn't choose to go into the Light, is because of that person's fear in what he or she believes will happen because of what he or she did prior to committing suicide. Meaning, because of what they believe will happen to them primarily because of the reason they committed suicide or because they may believe that God is going to punish them and they're going to go to hell.

I would never recommend suicide because of reasons later explained in this chapter, but if for some reason somebody reading this is thinking about it and is going to do it anyway, please choose to go into the Light. We are loved profoundly. I promise that the big hand of God won't come down and smash you to the ground with a closed fist. If, for any reason you might still be afraid to go into the Light, don't worry, because somebody will keep after you even if it lasts for thousands of years. We are all accounted for and it is important for us all, because of our interconnectedness to help wondering/ searching souls into the Light no matter how grim the soul's reality might be. One other thing I want to mention just in case any of you have lost a loved this way, is that your loved one is going to ultimately be okay and make it into the Light or what we would call here, the "other side." The other thing is, you can go to a shaman, psychic or somebody who is familiar with assisting souls into the Light. I will say this from my own experience of helping stuck souls into the Light, is that sometimes it can be a little bit of a challenge, mainly because of the soul's belief system. However, more often than not, there is victory, meaning they go into the Light. That being said, always know, that no matter what your belief system is or the belief system of the soul that committed suicide, the angels will never give up and never is a very long time!

We came to this planet with issues already existing in our consciousness even before we were born. These issues and concerns come from our past lives. Our parents and those circumstances that happen in our early childhood were simply reflections revealing the truth of what already existed inside of us, before we came here. So, if a person thinks it would be easier to commit suicide to set himself or herself free from past and present bondage, in order to finally feel happy, sorry, it won't work that way. We will just come right back to do it again, until we find Self-love and dissolve the illusions of separateness.

On that note, I highly recommend not to commit suicide. Although we won't go to hell for doing so, we might feel like we're in hell, because all of our issues will still be there. Hell is not a place we go if we do something bad when we die. It's a feeling of negative emotions, shame, guilt and fear.

If my soul is going to keep coming back over and over again until I learn these lessons I came here to learn, then why would I want to commit suicide? Why not move on and set myself free to the point where I may come back in a loving family and experience new forms of love that I never even knew existed? Think about that! Nothing happens to you. Everything happens for you. When I became aware of this, it gave me the incentive to be highly motivated to change my reality and stick around.

I have a dream to share with you. In the dream, it was nighttime and I had to walk through a fairground in order to get to my destination. As I was walking, I went past a Native American man. After passing him, I heard him shout to me, "Lance, come here!" I turned around, walked back toward him and stopped. We were standing about one foot away from each other. He leaned toward me, staring with strong intensity, deeply into my eyes and said, "You can have anything you want," as he handed me a red poker chip (representing to me that it was not a gamble). As I woke up from the dream, I knew beyond a shadow of a doubt that we can have anything we want. The reason I am sharing this dream is to reiterate the potential that lies in the technique I shared with you about asking the angels for help. That is an extremely powerful technique!

After all, just like here, souls do often change their perceptions on what they believe because the soul goes on and keeps learning forever.

A letter to my client about suicide

Dear Jain.
Sorry it took me so long to get back to you. I just want to let you know that, yes, your cousin did go into the Light. It is not your imagination that he went into the Light just to make you feel better. I have talked several people into the Light and that is exactly how I do it. So, you did a great job. No worries.

In God's eyes, there is nothing to forgive. There is nothing to judge. There is only unconditional love. Why would God look at his thumb and say, "I love my thumb, but I hate my thumbnail"? The reason it is so important for each one of us to be here and not to commit suicide, is because of our interconnectedness. When we learn something from our life experiences that sets us free, we are actually helping others through our interconnectedness. Now you can see how much we really do love one another, just by accepting the opportunity to be here on Earth. It is an honor to be here.

When people commit suicide, they do not go to hell, nor are they punished. The reason why they don't want to go into the Light is because of their self-inflicted fear of what they believe is going to happen to them if they enter that Light. Our beliefs and perceptions of realities are what create our experience when we choose to commit suicide. God does not do anything bad to us if we commit suicide; only our beliefs do.

If a person commits suicide and because of his or her beliefs winds up in a fear-based reality on the other side, that person will experience multiple opportunities to go into the Light. The soul that believes he or she is not worthy of going into the Light will eventually find help and make it. We live forever and forever is a long time. Nobody goes anywhere. We are all here. We are here to do our lessons, to free ourselves from the negative integrated beliefs from the past of others and our own false belief that we are separate from God. The only thing that committing suicide will do is give us a one-way ticket back Earth and to learn the lessons we've came here to learn all over again.

Committing suicide will not allow us to escape from the pain, sorrow, suffering and life situations that we came here to heal, feel and learn. The only way to escape is by diving in or going through our life's lessons and learning from them. It is then, that we can transmute what we have learned from the past into the purer forms of love and ultimately set ourselves free. We come here to break the chains of fear and to dissolve the diluted forms of love being expressed through our negative experiences and beliefs that we haven't let go of from our past, not only from this lifetime, but also from our past lives.

When we let go of these negative, diluted forms of love, we will then attract purer forms of love, which will be solidified into our consciousness. In so doing, we will assist in anchoring the heavenly realm here on planet Earth. Heaven on earth, goodwill toward men.

Heaven is not a place where we go when we die; heaven is a feeling. The "heavenly realm" that is commonly believed to be where we go when we die, is a vibration that coexists here on Earth. That is why we can speak to our angels and to our loved ones on the other side, because we are already on the other side. They're not up in the clouds somewhere far away; it's all here and now.

Many souls on Earth have a regimented, daily meditation practices incorporated into their lives. The daily practiced regiment of meditation will cause our energy to vibrate on higher frequencies, eventually matching the coexisting so-called heavenly realm's energies/frequencies. This will allow us to have increased communication with our loved ones, even to the point where there will no longer be a separation between the two realms.

In fact, this is happening now. As more and more people are raising their consciousness and becoming aware of their interconnectedness, meaning the Oneness, their combined resonating energies are causing the vibration of the planet to expand, as it's being altered through the ripple effect from the many who have raised their combined consciousness (meaning when two or more gather). The planet is being lovingly expanded and all that was hidden will be revealed.
Ascertaining these higher frequencies will ultimately help you vibrate in what many would call the heavenly realm frequencies, meaning the place we go when we die. By raising your frequencies through frequent meditation, it will cause you to be more psychic and make it easier to speak to loved ones on the other side.
Much love and many blessings! Lance

Helping loved ones into the Light

Sometimes when loved ones are ready to leave the earthly plane by aging or other means, they have a tendency to want to stick around. Oftentimes, I have had people call me and tell me how they see or feel the presence of their loved one still in their house.

When this happens, I give them this technique I use to help people into the Light. The main thing here is to never be afraid of a spirit of any kind. I like to think of a spirit like this: look at the person standing or sitting next to you and say "Boo!" because—guess what? They're just as much of a spirit as the one you can't see. The only difference is that the one standing or sitting next to you is in his or her body and the other one isn't.

When you speak to a spirit that is not in a body, it's exactly the same as talking to a person who is. All have their old belief systems and unique quirks. If for some reason you have a spirit in your house and you don't know who it is and it's just hanging around and you want it to leave, you can also use this same technique.

On some occasions, because of the spirit we assist into the Light may have fears of going into the Light and those fears can make it a bit of a challenge to help them. However, don't worry. Before I get started on helping the loved one go into the Light, I like to set up a preliminary procedure. How I do that is by using my mind's eye, also known as the third eye. I imagine another me, standing in front of me, with its hands extended straight out in front with palms out. Then I see a violet light coming down through the Crown chakra, bringing it through the heart and then pulling the violet, loving light out of my palms. Seeing it touching the spirit and visualizing a cocoon of that same violet light around the spirit. I then will call on Archangel Michael and he'll be more than happy to help you. The reason why I like to call on Archangel Michael, is because he can help on the other side to communicate with the spirit you're speaking to and he knows the spirit's beliefs better than you. He can use this knowledge to better convince the spirit to go into the light. The main thing here is not to worry about how or what Michael is doing, just know he is doing it.

Then, I will just start talking to the spirit just like I would if I were talking to a friend. It really helps to know a little about the beliefs of the spirit before you start. If you don't know, just use your intuition.

It will give you the right thing to say. One good thing to know is that most spirits are afraid to go into the Light because they think they did something wrong and that God is going to punish them. I like to start by telling the spirit not to worry, nothing bad is going to happen to them and that they will be safe, loved and that their loved ones are waiting for them on the other side. After I feel I have convinced the spirit to go into the Light, I then will say, "Look over to your left, there is an angel there. Do you see him?" I then pause, followed by, "Go ahead and walk up to the angel and take his hand. Do you see the Light there in front of you?" I pause for a little bit, then I tell the spirit that the angel is going to take them into the Light now and not to worry because everything is going to be fine. The main thing to know here, is that you don't have to say exactly the same words I use. If you get a feeling about something you need to say to try to convince the spirit into the Light, then say it. You can use your imagination. You may or may not see the spirit go into the Light. If you don't see the spirit going into the Light through your mind's eye, that is okay and there's nothing to worry about. You will know the spirit is gone, because of how your environment feels or all paranormal activity prior to helping the spirit into the Light will cease.

We have the power to tell any spirit or energy what to do or where to go. After all, if you integrate the Oneness into the equation, then, you are the spirit you are seeing or speaking to. So, what is it that you have to be afraid of? You are just speaking to an aspect of yourself that hasn't evolved to a higher state of consciousness yet. In fact, a lot of times, they're just coming to us for help.

If you're worried or scared about spirits being around you, then here's something that will really chap your hide. Even when you're sitting in a room talking to your friend about spiritual concepts, there could be hundreds or thousands of spirits all around, listening to every word you say and they are learning from you. The main thing here, is not to be afraid. You wouldn't be afraid if your grandmother came over to your house to pay a visit, would you? Here is a metaphor I like to use for individuals that may have a little fear about spirits and other aspects of the unknown. When the rattlesnake bites a rabbit, the rattlesnake doesn't say, "I'd better not eat that; there's poison in it." The rattlesnake embraces the poison it's eating and in doing so, the poison doesn't have any effect on the snake.

If you were to raise your awareness enough to the point where you believed that you were all things, you could eat anything, drink anything, be anywhere, touch anything, or even walk through a fire. Absolutely nothing would happen to you because you wouldn't be experiencing anything that wasn't you.

The power of God-Words

It is said that these words were the first words spoken in the creation of the universe. These words are more like commands in their most purist forms. This will be the only word that I will share with you, because of its ability to help the many, rather than the few. Each word received by an individual has a unique and alive-healing quality that, when spoken, can cause a mountain to move.

Before I explain what God-Words are and how you can obtain and use them, I would like to share a dream I had that helped me to become aware of their existence. Earlier, in chapter thirteen, I talked about a dream I had where I was walking through a big black slimy tunnel with a Tyrannosaurus Rex in it. One part I didn't mention was that in that dream, after taking a few steps forward, a door opened up on the right-hand side of the tunnel that allowed me to see into outer space. Suddenly, a spirit came floating up to the opening of the door as if it were going to come into the tunnel with me. I put my hands in front of me and said three times, "Eyataeway, Eyataeway, Eyataeway" and then repeated three times after, "Spirit be gone! Spirit be gone! Spirit be gone!" After going through this process, I immediately realized I translated what the word, "Eyataewa" means in my English language, which is, "Spirit be gone!"

I feel the reason they gave me this dream, not only to be aware of God-Words, they wanted me to discover that sometimes spirits from our past can play havoc and have a small amount of influence in this life. This made sense to me, considering we literally could be billions of years old and for the concept of non-separation. I think of it like this: We could be and are oftentimes, working old past life scenarios that involve spirits that are still on the other side. There is absolutely nothing to be afraid of. Rather, there is goodness. When you do become aware of a spirit messing around in your consciousness, you can use this word as a tool to send it on its way.

Here is an example of how I sent a spirit in human form away, when my wife and I were on a vacation in Canada. As we were waiting for a cab early in the morning, a man came up to us and asked for money. I gave him some money and he started getting belligerent and demanding more money. So, I just stuck my hand out in front of me, pointed it to him and said three times, "Eyataeway, Eyataeway, Eyataeway." Another guy sitting on the side of the road, yelled out like a great mighty trumpet, "LEAVE THEM ALONE!" The beggar just stopped, turned around and walked away.

I used this word once with a female client who came to me for healing. She told me she had a spirit inside of her. As I placed my hands on top of her head, I toned this same word (the word sounded out in a long continuous sound form) three times and all she did after I finished was shake around a little. When she stopped shaking, her eyes opened, she stood up like nothing ever happened and then, walked out of the office.

That goes to show you how powerful these words can be. The other words that are available, you'll have to get on your own, through your dreams. Normally, they are not meant to be shared with others, because of their unique activation properties within the individual they are given to. These words are considered to be sacred and are to be treated accordingly with respect and honor. Speaking of words and their use in communications, we can apply various techniques when communicating with and contacting our friends known as, extraterrestrials.

CHAPTER 17

How to make contact with our star-born ancestors

Often in sessions I am asked, "How can I get in touch with my star-born ancestors, ETs, or see UFOs? Before I answer this question, I would like to go over the process of how I was introduced to my star-born family. First, there can be a lot of fear in relation to this subject because of how ETs are depicted through the movie industry in a negative and threatening manner, when in fact, my experience has always been extremely loving, respectful and with integrity.

ETs are very concerned about scaring you and are very aware of your beliefs, so they will always take these things into consideration and will move extremely slow when it comes to contact. So don't worry about when you give them permission to make contact with you. It is possible in the next moment or days to come, they will just pop up and say, "Hi!" It is highly unlikely that will ever happen. For me, I didn't even consciously ask to know about ETs, but one night when sleeping, I had a dream where I was looking up in the sky and saw a huge spacecraft.

After the craft landed on the ground, a sphere about three feet in diameter with a big photo lens like an eye, came to me and followed me into a van. It started looking at me. Suddenly, the sphere left and went back to the spacecraft and that was when Archangel Michael came to me, took me by the hand and said, "Lance come with me." He introduced me to the ETs. About two years later, I had another dream of Archangel Michael and me, sitting in a restaurant, looking out the window at the clouds. I saw a UFO hidden in one of the clouds. I said to Michael,

"Do you see that UFO in the clouds?" Michael replied, "Yes, I do." That is when I realized that they could hide in the clouds and can even look like a cloud, but you can tell something is off. You can see the slightly darker shape of the UFO hidden within the cloud.

Asking for ET help

Each year, my visitation got a little stronger and stronger until one day, I was going through a rough time emotionally in my life and I realized I needed some help. I decided to ask my ET friends to help me. I told them that I was going up to Flagstaff, Arizona and that I would be camping overnight in the forest. I gave them permission to do whatever it takes to heal me. I figured I had nothing to lose, so that's why I asked them for help. I pitched my tent in a remote place in the woods and laid in my sleeping bag, waiting for them, until it got dark.

Suddenly, I noticed that my tent was lit up and I said to myself, "Why is my tent lit up, it's supposed to be night outside." I look to the left side of my tent and I saw two little ones approaching me, in the form of their shadows casted on the tent. I then said, "I see you!" All of a sudden, the tent got pitch dark only on that side. I began to notice a slight humming sound of a spaceship.

I realized I was both in and out of the ship at the same time and that I was being taken down a hallway on a gurney where they healed me with two different colored lights; red and green. I fell asleep. When I woke up the next morning, I felt like I could climb Mount Everest! I learned how they can control light at will. Later on, this awareness of their existence, led me to ask for an ET implant for a personal reason. When I received the implant, I felt even more peace and it became easier to communicate with them. The word implant scares many people because of what we hear in our media and believe to be truth. You don't have to worry though, because in order to get an implant or even a healing, you have to ask and give permission on some level to receive one.

There are some that say they were abducted by ETs and experienced a great deal of fear. I believe that is because the spirit of the person being taken on the spaceship, is the one that asked for the implant or healing to take place and the mind of the person has fears about what it is experiencing. This is perceived as something bad and creates chaos, whereas, the spirit of the person knows what is going on and is not afraid.

I have never had a bad experience with all types of ETs. They have always been extremely loving and respectful to me, my feelings and my beliefs. If we are afraid of this subject and our beliefs won't allow us to experience contact with our star-born ancestors, then it won't happen. We have to be willing to find the truth and seek the truth before contact of some sort can occur.

ET implants

I have had many contacts with my star-born ancestors in many forms and ways. Be open to the ways, without expectations and your dreams of knowing the truth and making contact, will come true and be worth your efforts. I will share with you the last of the many contact scenarios I have encountered. One day, I needed to get a magnetic resonance imaging (MRI) scan and I remembered I had implants in me. Some of you may know they are often made of a metallic substance and the metal will interfere with the imaging machine.

I told my ET family to please to take out my implants so I can get this MRI and put them back in after the procedure, because I have worked very hard to get those and don't want to lose them. Before I went to receive my MRI, my wife told me I was supposed to be there at six o'clock in the morning, when the office opened. I thought to myself, "Why in the heck, did my wife set up an appointment for me so early in the morning?!" I arrive at the office about fifteen minutes before the appointed time. I got out of the car and walked to the door to see the hours of operation. The sign said, "OPEN at 7am." I thought the facility opens at 7am, but my wife told me it opened at six!

I thought to myself, "Is she going crazy or what?" I went back to my car to sit and wait for an hour for them to open. I was sitting in the car for what felt like five minutes. A nurse came and opened the door. I thought, "What is she doing here so early?" I got out of the car and walked over to the door and read the sign again. This time the sign said, "WE OPEN at 6 am." I looked down at my watch to see what time it was. My watch said 6:00 am.

I thought, "What the hell! I was here at a quarter till six. The sign said, OPENS at 7am." I went back to my car to sit and wait until seven. I was only in my car for fifteen minutes. The nurse comes and opens the door. I get out of my car and read the sign once again. Instead of it saying OPENS at 7am, it now says, OPENS at 6am. I look again at my watch and it is 6 am, on the dot! I thought, "What the hell happened to the last hour? That was pretty good, what you guys did! But not that good, because you are so busted! You have to get up pretty early in the morning to fool me!"

No pun intended. I learned from this experience to pay attention to details. This is how to discover things that would normally be overlooked. They are masters of coming in and moving out, without us even knowing it. In fact, you who are reading this probably have had similar experiences because your soul is in cahoots with them and you have never even known it. I also learned that they could mess with what we would consider a firm and solid structure of time, which shows me that linear time only exists here on earth; to create structure and organization for chosen moments in time. When we look at the word, ancestors, to me that represents family. In my opinion, based on my personal life experience, there is nothing to be afraid of.

Wouldn't it be cool to meet other parts of your family? Just think of all the different ways to learn love, respect and integrity from people who are very loving and have been here for a very long time.

It can be a challenge to learn these perspectives here on Earth because we live by the laws of the earthly perspective. I am so grateful that we can have the opportunity if we choose, to learn deeper perspectives of love, joy, respect, integrity, happiness and many different types of our inherent abilities, from our star-born ancestors. I have felt and experienced unlike anything I have experienced here on Earth, the deepest trust, respect, love and integrity from my star-born ancestors. I have learned we are capable of so much more then we have been made and chose to believe in, living here on Earth. We can experience and have opportunities way beyond our wildest dreams and imaginations. It's our individual choice. We are all in this together. It's not them up there and us down here. It's us, all here together, as family working together, for the greater good of all man and womankind.

Technique: how to establish contact with ETs

Start by deep and slow breathing into your spine, primarily using your abdominal muscles, as the primary means of breathing. See your spine light up like a neon light and while breathing in the light, the light gets brighter. Think of your breath as the source of power for the light you are sustaining. After breathing about five times into the spine, then see a beam of light coming from the spine going to the heart and illuminating the heart chakra. Then start breathing into your physical heart. Generate and feel the love expanding into your heart. Breath into your heart until you feel the love expanding out your heart as strong as possible. Now expand your love in the form of light out from your spine and your heart, out into infinite space. Then, with your imagination, see a funnel of your clockwise spinning pristine love and light, coming out from the top of your head and going straight up into infinite space. Keep breathing slowly and deeply feeling and seeing yourself as a radiant beacon of light. When you feel really connected to the love and the universe inside of you, say inside or out loud, "I am giving permission for my star-born ancestors to make contact with me in infinite forms of communication."

I recommend not having preconceived thoughts of what you think or how they will communicate to you, because that is equivalent to putting your intentions in a box. After all, we are where we are, in the moment and that is as far as our perception allows us to experience our contact. There are many different ways how they can contact us, so I recommend giving them open range, so that we can have the experience of contact no matter what form it comes in. This way, we can grow from there. Think of it like this: when we go to college and it is our first day at school, we haven't got a clue of how the teacher is going to teach us or the process of how we are going to be taught or what is to be presented to us. After we experience a few days of class, then things start to make sense and we start to see the bigger picture. Contact works the same way.

After using this contact technique for about a month, something really wonderful happened for me. I started seeing geometric patterns, very faint profile images of ETs, spaceships would fly in to my mind's eye and stop right in the middle of my vision, so that I could get a good look at them. Remember, there is nothing to be afraid of when establishing contact with your star-born ancestors, because they will go very slow at first. It took me years to get to the point where I'm at now.

The Plejarens are here!

After a few weeks of different ways of contact my friend Barbra Becker, the QHHT® practitioner/regression hypnotherapist, called me and tells me about the experience of a good friend of ours, Zaysan Saldausky. He likes to be called, Z. I call him by his native name I made up for him, "The better looking one." Barbara told me that she was editing a book which is actually Z's diary from his current ongoing experiences with the star-born people called, Plejarens. Barbara told me Z's encounter with these people was only going to be allowed to be shared by a very small group of people, so fortunately and with great gratitude, I was included in that group.

Barbara and I would talk for long periods of time about what Z was experiencing in his daily contact experience. One time, when Barbara read several chapters to me and we got off the phone, I thought to myself, "Oh My God! This book/diary is actual contact! Wow!" I thought, "How lucky I was to even know about this book and be one of the humans included to read it!" I realized this book is "hot off the press" and ongoing in real time. I thought to myself, "What an opportunity to finally learn the truth." I mean, think about this, no black lines hiding the words, not coming from what we have been fed for centuries now and the most loving way to express themselves, the Plejarens interact with respect and transparency. Wow, what a concept! Is it possible to have interaction with ETs, in this manner? Well guess what? The council members of the Plejarens read Z's diary and realized how important it was to let everybody read this book, not just five people in the whole world. This book holds information that would normally be hidden deep in a temple, somewhere, for certain eyes only. Thank God, the Plejarens gave Z permission to publish the book.

I highly recommend if you are serious about learning the most up to date truth about our star-born ancestors, go to Amazon.com or Kindle.com and buy the books. Two of the three book series have been published. When you purchase the books, one hundred percent of the book royalties fund the rescue of children from sex slavery, all over the world, through Z's non-profit organization, www.thequestecss.org. In other words, your money is helping children be rescued, purchasing of medical treatment, food, clothing and education supplies, in newly created orphanages, where they thrive in their loving and supportive community with other children that have gone through the same experiences.

The first book is, *Plejaren Diaries: Accidental Contact*
The second book is, *Plejaren Diaries: Interstellar Divinity*

Be patient with yourself

Before I end my book, please keep in mind that everybody has a different time frame for shifting their consciousness to a new level. There are all kinds of reasons why some things take years to happen or can magically take seconds. The speed of our healing all depends on how much our soul has already processed. Just remind yourself when doing any type of healing modality, be it, meditation, Self-love techniques, letting go of the past, ceremonies, whatever you use to heal, be patient with yourself. Patience is a form of Self-love. The only ones that say hurry up and get it, is us. If you chose to do anything that is in this book or anything that is not and use it to heal yourself, please don't get frustrated if you have to do something over several times before it takes hold, by all means, do it. It is not a waste of time. No matter what modality you choose because of its resonance with you, or which healer you go to, I can guarantee, you will receive a very important healing. When you receive a healing, it may or may not happen the way you expected the healing to happen. That, in no way, means you didn't receive a profound healing or a healing didn't take place. Sometimes the things we want to be healed from, are more at the surface, than other facets of what we are working on. The ones that are closer to the surface of our consciousness, can oftentimes go away very fast, like magic. Other issues that are more in the background, or at the beginning of our internal discovery, can be set in motion to start their process of leaving, or being transmuted. They will take a little longer. So be patient and loving with yourself and allow your unique process to take place in its own space and time, without any self-judgment.

Much love and many blessings to all.
Lance

About the Author

Lance Heard was born with his inherent shamanistic abilities. At a very young age and for several years of his childhood, he would spend several hours a week out in the desert constantly asking for answers to his questions. Although Lance had difficulties coping with his internal struggles based on his chosen path this lifetime, freedom came when he discovered and accepted that without the pain, he wouldn't have had the incentive to find the pristine inner happiness and love, he so desired. Just this very awareness in itself, caused him to step out of his self-created box and utilize his inherent abilities.

Throughout Lance Heard's creative process, he discovered many modalities that he used to help and assist himself, which translated into him writing this book in the hope of possibly helping others. In his spiritual practice, Lance offers many healing opportunities, such as hands-on healing, Reiki, energetic advancement consultation, ceremonies, meditation techniques and dream interpretation.

If you're interested in learning more about Lance and his services, please contact him at lanceheard.com.

RECOMMENDED REGRESSION HYPNOTHERAPIST

Barbara Becker, R.N. ret., CHt.

Retired Critical Care Registered Nurse
IACT Certified Hypnotherapist
QHHT® (Quantum Healing Hypnosis Technique)
BQH (Beyond Quantum Healing online hypnosis)
Past-life regression

https://www.barbarabeckerenergy.com

Made in the USA
Middletown, DE
13 February 2023

23967857R00089